Imperium Press was founded in 2018 to supply students and laymen with works in the history of rightist thought. If these works are available at all in modern editions, they are rarely ever available in editions that place them where they belong: outside the liberal weltanschauung. Imperium Press' mission is to provide right thinkers with authoritative editions of the works that make up their own canon. These editions include introductions and commentary which place these canonical works squarely within the context of tradition, reaction, and counter-Enlightenment thought—the only context in which they can be properly understood.

ANTHROPOMORPHICS

AN ORIGINARY GRAMMAR
OF THE CENTER

DENNIS BOUVARD

PERTH
IMPERIUM PRESS
2020

Published by Imperium Press

www.imperiumpress.org

© Dennis Bouvard, 2020
The moral rights of the author have been asserted
Used under license to Imperium Press

FIRST EDITION

A catalogue record for this
book is available from the
National Library of Australia

ISBN 978-0-6486905-7-3 Paperback
ISBN 978-0-6486905-8-0 EPUB
ISBN 978-0-6486905-9-7 Kindle

CONTENTS

ACKNOWLEDGEMENTS

I would first off like to thank *Imperium Press* for their interest in my book. It has been a pleasure working with their editor.

I would also like to thank Chris Bond, whose blog, *Reactionary Future*, was very helpful to me as I was working through my critique of liberalism, and who has provided encouragement and collaboration, while making concrete contributions to improving the manuscript. I hope this book and his *Nemesis* will be read together.

I also thank Joel Davis and Imperius for sustained and challenging intellectual engagement with, and dissemination of, my work and, most of all, doing the kind of legwork and networking I can only imagine so as to produce an audience for the book. I doubt whether I would have written it without the potential readership that, largely thanks to them, I can now hope for.

Also, thanks to everyone on the *Postliberalism* Discord server, who have been giving GA a real basis in the social world. I'm looking forward to seeing what they, and those they inspire, do with these ideas.

And, of course, I wish to express my gratitude to Eric Gans, above all for his still astonishing "originary hypothesis," which has guided my intellectual pursuits for around two decades now, while I still feel like I'm just getting started; but also for maintaining, almost singlehandedly, the online journal *Anthropoetic*s, and for hosting the *GABlog* on his *Anthropoetics* website, which gave me space to develop many of the ideas in this book.

ANTHROPOMORPHICS

A BRIEF INTRODUCTION

This book unfolds what I see as the most powerful potentials of the originary hypothesis of the origin of language and humanity proposed by Eric Gans. It might help the reader to keep in mind a couple of methodological principles distinguishing the mode of writing here from what you might see in most theoretical works. First, rather than comparing the "picture" of the world implicit in the originary hypothesis to similar pictures produced by other theories and trying to measure their respective adequacy to a shared reality from some presumably neutral standpoint, I work under the assumption that the power of a theory lies in its entry into language, or various discursive spaces, such as to convert those spaces into the kind of originary reflection called for by the hypothesis. Second, it follows (and this only became clear to me in the course of writing) that this mode of writing must project a world in which everyone has adopted, or will eventually have adopted, the originary hypothesis and re-purposed their attention and disciplinary spaces[1] accordingly. The way we would all be coming to speak of things if we were all in the process of incorporating the originary hypothesis and all its implications is the way, I find, I am speaking here. So, the reader is thrown *in medias res*, with regular recallings of the beginnings in the middle. It is an attempt to think outside of, so as to re-enter strategically, what I call (following David Olson) the meta-language of literacy. You

---

1 By "disciplinary space" I will mean any shared use of language insofar as it aims at ensuring everyone there is seeing the same thing at the same time.

are already thinking in originary terms of the center, and so let's think together of how we are doing so and how to do so more explicitly—that is my address to the reader.

Let me put it another way, drawing upon what I see as a seminal distinction within originary thinking, a distinction made by Gans in his *The End of Culture*, between "producer's desire" and "consumer's satisfaction":

> In the original scene of representation, the members of the community, in designating their object, at the same time imaginarily prolong their act of designation into the originally intended act of appropriation. But this imaginary act aims at the possession, no longer merely of an object of appetitive satisfaction, but of the unique significant referent of the designating gestures of the entire community, This desire, absolute and unfulfillable, is the model of what we might call "producer's desire".
>
> The scene of representation terminated, each member of the community acts to appropriate his own portion of the object. Now the appetitive goal is subsumed within a desire for participation along with the others in the significance that has just been conferred on the object. We may call this "consumer's satisfaction." The unsustainable desire for the whole is compensated for by participation in collective appropriation where each receives an equivalent share. (158)

Gans is here referring to a dichotomy between two moments on the originary scene itself, but is doing so in the context of the emergence of the "Big Man," who, in the archaic community, distinguishes himself by retrieving producer's desire and "usurping" the center. This move on the part of the Big Man, which, as Gans goes on to say, "takes a major step beyond the ritual leaders of egalitarian society toward the divinization that will be the lot of the ancient monarchs" (159), is an exceptional act of deferral in order to distribute. But the desire informing the act is the possession of the unique significance of the central object, even if that desire, "in its most radical sense, can never be fulfilled" (160). Producer's desire is necessarily prior to consumer's satisfaction, but, since consumer's satisfaction "takes [the community's] existence for granted" (160), clear, comprehensive, "packaged," "naturalized" and pacified portrayals of social order represent the standpoint of the consumer. It is this standpoint from which all contenders for power presently claim to speak precisely so that they can plausibly claim to represent what is stable in the social order. This book is written to support the "praxis" of producer's desire, which "must be *integrated into* the community" (160, italics in original) precisely because it is engaged in producing the significant center which makes order possible. The praxis of producer's desire is a praxis of world creation through language, that is, through the appropriation of language and its naming capacity.

Everything in this book is hypothetical—the book itself is a sustained hypothesis. All language use is hypothetical—every utterance is a hypothesis regarding the possible responses and consequences of the utterance. The originary hypothesis of Eric Gans suggests as much, both in affirming that one can only hypothesize regarding origins, especially of language and the human, and in hypothesizing that language emerged in a necessarily uncertain effort to defer violence. Some hypotheses are better than others, though. Not because they can be "proven," though, as proof has nothing to do with the social sciences—the more you try to restrict the "variables" on the model of the physical sciences the more you create artificial conditions from which any extrapolation is useless. The better hypothesis is the one that people can stand in for and enrich and further represent the social relations implicit in the hypothesis. A better hypothesis, that is, provides its users with ways of rendering their practices more hypothetical, and therefore more dependent on attending to the conditions of their articulation. You could also call this "faith," or the kind of faith in which the faithful are always seeking that difference in every act that would pertain especially to their relation to God. The better hypothesis, like the better faith, is the one that can inhabit and convert the most discourses, activating them as if they were on the verge of enacting the hypothesis already.

II

THE USE OF A CENTER

> Act so that there is no use in a centre.
> Gertrude Stein

If you act so that there is no use in a center, your action would be dissolving all possible, all imaginable, uses in a center. If there's a center, you can be equidistant from it with others; you can be closer to it or more distant from it than others. A center establishes a hierarchy—at the very least between center and margin. But every other hierarchy is modeled on the hierarchy between center and margin—hierarchies are only possible if there is a center. Presumably, that's why Stein would enjoin us to act so that there is no use in a center, but following her imperative would place her injunction at the center as we take her as a model for detecting, identifying and then disabling this use of the center, that use, and then other uses. But in thus acting to dissolve the center, we would need to use the center, at least in order to determine which use of it requires the most urgent attention. So, as we subtract uses, we add uses to the center: acting so that there is no use in a center is, in fact, a discovery procedure for revealing and naming all the uses of a center.

In Jacques Derrida's "Structure, Sign and Play in the Human Sciences," we are given and warned about a great many uses of the center. The center allows for the "structurality of structure"; it provides a "fixed point of origin"; it allows for "free play within the system," which depends upon the "coherence" provided by a center; it also limits the free play within the system (allowing and limiting free play may be two different, not incompatible, uses). But, according to "classical thought" concerning structure:

> the center is, paradoxically, *within* the structure and *outside* it. The center is at the center of the totality, and yet, since the center does not belong to the totality (is not part of the totality), the totality *has its center elsewhere*. The center is not the center. The concept of centered structure—although it represents coherence itself, the condition of the epistémé as philosophy or science—is contradictorily coherent. And, as always, coherence in contradiction expresses the force of a desire. The concept of centered structure is in fact the concept of a play based on a fundamental ground, a play which is constituted upon a fundamental immobility and a reassuring certitude, which is itself beyond the reach of the play. And on the basis of this certitude anxiety can be mastered, for anxiety is invariably the result of a certain mode of being implicated in the game, of being caught by the game, of being as it were at stake in the game from the outset. And again on the basis of what we call the center (and which, because it can be either inside or outside, can also indifferently be called the origin or end, *arché* as *telos*), the repetitions, the substitutions, the transformations, and the permutations are always *taken* from a history of meaning [sens]—that is, in a word, a history—whose origin may always be reawakened or whose end may always be anticipated in the form of presence. This is why one could perhaps say that the movement of any archeology, like that of any eschatology, is an accomplice of this reduction of the structurality of structure and always attempts to conceive of structure on the basis of a full presence which is beyond play. (279, italics in original)

Derrida's language here seems strangely intentionalistic and even psychologistic at crucial points. The center holds the structure together, and is therefore inside the structure; but, the center is not subject to the free play of elements within the structure, and is therefore outside of the structure. This paradox, or "coherence in contradiction," "expresses the force of a desire." This is a desire for certitude, a mastering of anxiety—it is a way of establishing a teleology, wherein the end is contained in the origin. The center is presumably fragile as well—otherwise, why the anxiety?—and, therefore, a challenge to one center is met through a series of substitutions and permutations, a constant decentering, with one center replacing another. Still the logic here seems to be progressive, insofar as each decentering implicates the new center further in the free play it sought to avoid, and we become increasingly aware of our implication in the game. (It's not clear whether this makes us more or less anxious.) The watershed here seems to be when "language invaded the universal problematic," implicating all centers in the play of differences.

What prevents us from moving from "metaphysics" to "discourse," in that case? Why is it that "*[t]here is no sense* in doing without the concepts of metaphysics in order to attack metaphysics. We have no language—no syntax and no lexicon—which is alien to this history; we cannot utter a single destructive proposition which has not already slipped into the form, the logic, and the implicit postulations of precisely what it seeks to contest"? It is interesting that the example Derrida provides demonstrating why "we have not language" is the concept of the "sign" itself, which we cannot do without but which Derrida contends is unthinkable without the metaphysical distinction between "sensible" and "intelligible." We can take the concept of the sign, then, as a test for whether we can have any language, not necessarily "alien to this history" but inclusive of and non-reducible to it. We can agree with Derrida that the sign belongs at the center of the human sciences, precisely because the sign marks the threshold of the human. Whether we speak in terms of a Peircean "symbol," or the distinction between signifier and signified, the sign is different from any form of non-human communication insofar as the operation of any sign is both conventional and historical while being outside of conventionality and history. Words only mean what they mean insofar as a community of language users "agrees" that that is what they mean; but the word "agree" is clearly inadequate because a community, as was perhaps first pointed out by Rousseau, would already have to have language to "agree" on the meaning of signs. But this means that the origin of language would also be the origin of community and, indeed, the origin of the human. Derrida's intuition regarding the paradoxicality of any such origin, or any attempt to posit an origin, is formidable;

and his failure or refusal to hypothesize regarding an origin more originary than any other is unsurprising.

Derrida's intuition regarding the articulation of "center," "origin," "desire" and "anxiety" is also remarkable. Something like "desire" and something like "anxiety" would, indeed, have to lie at the origin of the sign, because the sign articulates attention, and desire and anxiety both sharpen and singularize attention. Where there is attention, there is a center of that attention. As Michael Tomasello has pointed out, the apparently very simple activity of pointing or, more specifically, "pointing something out," is something only humans do. What Tomasello calls "joint attention" is constitutive of human sign use, and is intimately linked to the paradoxical "agreement" discussed in the previous paragraph.[1] We are each directing the other's attention to something, and also showing each other that we know the other is doing so. The paradoxicality and recursivity definitive of human language is already present on this simple scene: nothing but our respective gestures toward some center sustains the gestures themselves, but for each of us the gesture is always already available—neither of us invented it or could imagine it to have been "invented" (or "discovered"). It only remains to produce a hypothesis regarding the possibility of this paradoxical construct.

---

1 I would suggest his *The Origins of Human Communication* as the best introduction to Tomasello's work.

III

ORIGIN
AND HYPOTHESIS

There already is such a hypothesis, and has been for forty years; this hypothesis is the starting point of this book, and following its implications, or at least one set of implications, will be its subject matter. The originary hypothesis, advanced by Eric Gans in his *The Origin of Language* in 1981 (and subsequently revised and clarified over a series of books),[1] posits a singular event within which language, or the sign, originates. Gans's starting point is Rene Girard's understanding of the conflictual nature of mimesis: as humans are the most mimetic species, and mimesis generates rivalry because our model, the more we model ourselves on him, becomes our rival for the same object, mimesis leads to crisis, in which the continued existence of the community can be at stake. Girard's hypothesis is that in some such crisis of a "proto-human" species of hominid, a single member of the group is "marked" and singled out as the source of the mimetic contagion, with this "scapegoat" then murdered by the rest of the group. The mimetic frenzy of undifferentiation is thereby "discharged" upon this single "absolutely" different member. The scapegoat then becomes the first divine being, insofar as he has "saved" the community.

Gans sees the outcome of the originary event differently. The limit of Girard's account is that there is no reason for the event in

1   I will focus particularly on *The End of Culture* (1985), *Science and Faith* (1990) and *Originary Thinking* (1993), but see the bibliography for a full list of Gans's work. His ongoing *Chronicles of Love & Resentment*, found on his *Anthropoetics* website, and now numbering well over 600, further clarify and extend Gans's understanding of the originary hypothesis.

question to become meaningful and memorable. Why should the killing of a conspecific, not a very unusual event among mammals, transform the group in any way? I used the word "murder" in my description of the scene, but "murder" presupposes a moral order, and nothing in Girard's scenario accounts for how the scene would create such an order. This is another way of saying that Girard doesn't account for the emergence of language, which would itself be a prerequisite of a moral order and a community to share it. For Gans, the hypothetical scene is revised as follows. Gans assumes that the mimetic crisis is organized around some object of appetitive attention—most likely some food source, perhaps a recent kill. Ordinarily, among the higher primate species, the object would be consumed in order, first by the Alpha animal, then by the Beta, and so on. But on this occasion, the mimetic rivalry induced by the object overrides the pecking order as all members of the group move toward the object at the center. Appetite becomes "desire," that is, a social phenomenon involving one's relation to others and not merely the object itself. Desire intensifies the mimetic crisis. However, within the group, some member hesitates, presumably out of something like terror ("anxiety" would not be quite right here), is seen by others to hesitate, and is imitated by others. The gesture indicates a renunciation, perhaps momentary (but that is enough), of the desired object. This, what Gans calls "the gesture of aborted appropriation," is the first sign. The rivalrous imitation that first propels the group toward the center and potentially cataclysmic violence is converted into a pacifying imitation that de-escalates the crisis; the order provided by the animal pecking order is replaced by an order mediated by the sign, which defers violence through representation. A new species is born: the human, the only species, as Gans puts it, that poses a greater danger to its own survival than is posed to it by anything in its environment.

The first sign is an ostensive sign—that is, it is inextricable from the event in which it is issued and therefore constitutes the object it refers to. But this is not an act of existential free will on the part of each member of the new community. None of them could articulate such a will, not only because they have no language in which to do so, but because the sign cannot be attributed to an intentionality "internal" to any of the members of the group.

Each is only repeating the others' reference to the central object—none of them could be the origin. And yet intention has been introduced into the community, in the form of the object itself. As the participants on the scene see each other sharing attention to the object of desire, the only agency that could be holding them back is the potential victim itself. The creation of the human is mediated by the creation of the sacred center as the creator of the human.

The victim does need to be consumed, and the emergent community does need to put its new sign to work to ensure this can be done in a communal and non-violent (or, sufficiently non-violent so that the mimetic crisis is not re-activated) manner. In the sparagmos, the tension generated by the prior restraint is released, and so this danger does present itself as the community attacks the meal in this unprecedented manner. Resentment at the object itself, for imposing restraint and refusing itself, intensifies the devouring of the body. The only thing preventing each member from overreaching his bounds and turning on his fellows is the sign itself, which we can imagine working within the sparagmos as a kind of reminder of the collective limits making this peaceful consumption possible. Following the sparagmos, as the members of the community face each other over the remains of their victim/meal/deity, the sign would be issued once again, this time pointing to the remainders and mementos of the sacred being, marking the first ritual. Naturally, this hypothetical account in fully developed language that is both unavailable to the participants on the scene and marked by the limitations of constructing the emergence of language from within language, must present coherently a sequence that might have developed over a series of similar events—and, more importantly, might be reconstructed for memory through more orderly rituals. The value of such an account, though, lies in the need to hypothesize the sign being repeated, made memorable, and acting generatively within the community. Eventually the ritual would be moved to prior to the act of consumption, so as to prevent in advance the possibility that this time the scene might not play out in ideal form.

The paradoxes of deferral we see on the originary scene are enduring features of the human. That which we desire and which therefore thrusts itself upon our attention, is given excess desirability through our mimetic relations with our fellows—desiring something is inseparable from imagining others desiring it. For this very reason we are forbidden our object of desire, as we intuit the violence implicit in our approach to it. And yet, we might be granted our desire, insofar as our satisfaction is mediated through the cultural (sign) systems that allot desirable objects in such a way as to build layers of deferral that themselves keep at bay the need to improvise means of deferral in dire circumstances (which circumstances, nevertheless, on occasion occur). The alienation of our desires must be represented to us, and we must receive our desired object as a gift from the center. The fact that many take short cuts and evade or violate the cultural mechanisms that formalize our satisfactions as an exchange with the center doesn't contradict this claim—rather, it explains our resentment towards those transgressors and our marking them as "criminal" or "immoral." The immoral and criminal must tell themselves, meanwhile, that their own exceptional relation to the center, due to unique circumstances or unusual abilities, authorizes a form of appropriation forbidden to others. Our most immediate desires throw us into a net of social obligations.

IV

A GRAMMAR OF THE
SOCIAL

Gans, in *The Origin of Language*, hypothesizes in a remarkably thorough and precise manner the development of the more developed speech forms out of the original ostensive sign. I will present this development here in what can be no more than an outline form, while returning to the sequence of speech forms in new contexts throughout my discussion. Following the ostensive is the imperative. The imperative is a result of an "inappropriate ostensive." One member of the community issues the ostensive sign in the absence of the object, and another member of the community then supplies the object. Gans is solving a very important problem in this hypothesis of the creation of the imperative. Note that the problem of accounting, not just for the emergence of language, but its development from its earliest forms, is that any intention or "motivation" we might attribute to these early language users is going to presuppose that they already possess the more advanced form we are trying to explain. So, to explain the imperative as a result of someone "wanting someone else to provide him with an object," seemingly the simplest motivation imaginable, would already presuppose the availability of the imperative. Note that the originary hypothesis accounts for the issuing of the first sign by constructing an attentional space that is first of all convergent, and therefore dangerous, and then becomes shared—in this way, we can see attention becoming intention without anyone actually intending for this to happen.

Similarly, in accounting for the imperative, the sign has to become iterable, memorable and deployable without anyone intending for this to happen. So, we imagine, perhaps, an inexperienced sign user, perhaps a child, imitating "blindly" a gesture she has seen others make; another member of the community, perhaps an adult but still unable to conceive of a sign used "improperly," "redeems" the sign by providing its missing referent. I will note now that this "method" of accounting for the emergence of new linguistic and cultural forms as a result of a "mistake" that is then "retrieved" within the community is central to originary thinking. Gans introduces the concept needed for us to motivate this act of retrieval: "linguistic presence." What participants in a sign community desire above all is the maintenance of linguistic presence: any scene we are on must be mediated by signs, and if we intuit that some element of a particular scene is going unrepresented, we treat that as a danger to be remedied through the application of a sign. So, a mistaken use of a sign opens a kind of rupture on the scene that must be recuperated somehow—this can be done by "marking" the "guilty" party, but it can also be done by granting a new meaning to the mistaken sign on the terms of the scene itself. I will point to another element of originary thinking illustrated by Gans's derivation of the imperative that I will also be returning to—the emergence of linguistic and cultural forms from marginal sites within the community. So, if one were to pose the question, "how might the imperative have emerged within a community of sign users who only had access to ostensive signs?" a more obvious or commonsensical attempt to answer it might look to relations of power and authority within the community: we might imagine, for example, an adult who "wants" to command a child to do something. The reverse is much more likely the case: forms that emerge marginally through mistakenness[1] are then appropriated within and help to formalize the existing power relations within the community: once the imperative is in use, someone in a position to do so can "want" to command another.

In moving directly from the ostensive to the imperative, I skipped over an important development that lays the ground work for that leap into a new linguistic form. Once the originary sign has been issued within the event, on the scene, there is no obvious reason to assume that it will be used outside of that

---

1 See my "Originary Mistakenness, Defilement and Modernity," in *Anthropoetics*, XVI, No. 1, Fall 2010.

very controlled situation. In other words, we can readily imagine, for quite a while, everything else remaining the same within that group: they hunt the same way, gather the same way, mate the same way, battle with competing "packs" the same way, while only issuing the sign within the ritualized framework of approaching their meals. The originary sign creates a radical difference between the meaningful central object, on the one hand, and everything else, on the other. Still, we can't imagine this continuing indefinitely, because in the sign the group has a means of deferring violence, and the need to defer violence must occur in varied settings. Indeed, once it is known that certain dangerous situations can be prevented, it becomes possible to identify potentially dangerous situations, albeit somewhat less dangerous than that of the originary scene, and to issue the sign in such situations. This is the way in which new objects and acts would come to be named, and signs differentiated from each other. Gans refers to this process as one in which the "threshold of significance" is continually lowered, and more of the world is made representable. The use of the sign outside of its ritual constraints would be an instance of scandalous "secularization," one for which we could imagine the sign user paying some price; a re-issuance of the original sign, with its higher degree of sacrality, within this new context would recuperate this unwarranted usage within the evolving language system. The community could recognize its belonging to the same salvationist project.

We should view the ostensive and the imperative as comprising a pair. For an imperative to be completed, and to therefore be meaningful, an object must actually be supplied: the supplying of the object is recognized, at least tacitly, with a confirming ostensive (Gans here uses the example of an operating room, in which the doctor calls for the "scalpel" with the single word command, with the nurse providing it along with the confirming "scalpel.") At the same time, the imperative makes more explicit the "command" implicit in any ostensive. An object pointed to, referred to, named, is thereby protected, at the very least insofar as we are enjoined to observe rather than appropriate it. The injunction to defer appropriation issued by the central being on the originary scene already has the elements of a command: something like "stay your hand!" The world of objects, and each singularized or identified object, similarly issues such a command, which is not a command to refrain from consumption or use indefinitely, but to refrain from any consumption or use that is not already sanctioned in the very name of the object in question. The uses that are sanctioned by any ostensive sign are determined by its origin and subsequent recuperation with the sign and cultural system. What Gans calls the "dialectic of the imperative" begins with the observation that while, for the one issuing the imperative, the imperative is in effect an ostensive (for the "imperator" the object is as good as present) for the one obeying the imperative, the space of the other's desire is opened up. A new form of reciprocity becomes possible and necessary. Some imperatives are perhaps unproblematic, but for those that aren't, and that threaten to break linguistic presence and initiate new conflicts, the preservation or restoration of linguistic presence would involve deriving the imperative from the object demanded or, more broadly, the world of objects, which is to say, the central being constituting that world. Every ostensive-imperative articulation adds to the repertoire of the center, whether an imperative is issued in the name of God, of reality or exigency.

We don't have "reality" yet, in the sense of a world of objects separate from the sign users themselves. Ostensives and imperatives rely upon the presence of the referent of the sign, and of the sign users to each other. We can take Derrida's lesson that there is no unmediated presence by pointing out that central being presides over all linguistic acts without being indexical within them. To more fully address Derrida's critique of logocentrism, though, we will need to finish working through the succession of speech forms, because the cogency of Derrida's concept relies upon the way meaning is articulated in the declarative speech form. The declarative emerges in response to a problem raised by the imperative—what we might call, although Gans doesn't, an "inappropriate imperative." There would be imperatives that couldn't be fulfilled, raising the specter of a breakdown of linguistic presence. In some cases, the one issuing the imperative would "let it go," either due to the unimportance of the request or the inability to enforce the command. But what if a more complex situation emerges—an imperative is not complied with, but it's not clear that it can't be complied with; the one issuing the imperative may not be able to enforce it, but, then again, the probability of doing so may seem high enough to risk pressing the point, even if not past a certain, as yet undetermined, point. So, the imperative is repeated—let's say first with more urgency, as the "gambit" or bluff is played; then with a degree of uncertainty, as the imperator "climbs back down," but not completely. In this latter case, the imperative is prolonged, along with a tonal shift—the imperative becomes an interrogative, implicitly allowing for some response from the one being issued the imperative.

The problem of linguistic presence is now posed in a new way. The stakes of the situation have been lowered—at this point, it's clear that no physical confrontation is imminent—but that makes the situation all the riper for innovation. In other words, it is one of those marginal, mistaken sign usages wherein a new form can emerge. The recipient of what is now a question has the opportunity to "inform" his interlocutor that the requested object is not available. Again, though, the interlocutor can't simply "want" to "offer information," because the speech form in which such a desire could be formulated is precisely what is about to be invented. First of all, the name of the object requested is repeated, as in an ostensive-imperative articulation—this maintains linguistic presence. The name, what is about to become the "substantive," ("topic" or "subject") is about to be conjoined with the "comment" ("predicate") upon that topic/subject. The comment is derived from a linguistic act Gans refers to as the "operator of negation," which is a form of the imperative but one somewhat abstracted from the conditions of presence in which we have so far found the imperative. The operator of negation is a more open-ended imperative forbidding some action. Gans gives the example of "don't smoke," which is an imperative that can never actually be fulfilled—it's always possible that at some future time the one so forbidden to will light up. More obvious examples would be the "Thou Shalt Nots" of the Ten Commandments: we will never have finished not committing murder.[2]

It's not clear how such open-ended prohibitions have emerged within the language of ostensives and imperatives we are presupposing here. It's noteworthy that such prohibitions involve

2 I'm working here with the material in chapters 13 and 14, pages 93-104, of the (far more accessible new [2019]) edition of *The Origin of Language*.

refraining from some action, rather than the provision of a desired object, which has been the kind of imperative we have been looking at so far. Telling someone not to do something seems to already presuppose the availability of declarative sentences, since it seems dependent upon representing the act to be forbidden. So, we need an operator of negation that would precede an explicit formulation of an act—a more primitive form of the operator of negation, in other words. We can have recourse here to the originary sign, which, insofar as it refers to the central object, sacralizes that object but, insofar as it is directed to the other participants, issues a kind of injunction, and prohibits a very specific act. All we need is the possibility of a sign that is the equivalent of "do not," split off, so to speak, from the originary sign. The reference to the specific act in question would always be context bound.

So, we have the repetition of the name of the object demanded along with something like "don't…" as our proto-declarative. It seems to me that we still need to account for how the operator of negation is to be taken as a "comment," which is to say something said "about" the object which has been requested. After all, it's still in the form of an imperative, which must be addressed to… whom, exactly? Most directly, it would seem to be addressed to the object, which is mentioned along with it—commanding it to refrain from making itself present. More intuitively, though, it would seem to be addressed to the other, commanding him to refrain from persisting in the request. The innovation, though, would be found in the counter-intuitive treatment of the command as issued to the object—that an object is not there because it has been ordered off the scene represents a new possibility. But this command, while uttered by the target of the request, could not originate with him—after all, if he was able to order the object off the scene, he presumably could have supplied it in the first place. The first time that "information" was offered, then, was not in the form of a "statement of fact," but in a command by an Other to establish a "reality" immune to the desires of both interlocutors. I would say that such a command could only be assumed to come from the central object, or sacred Being. (At this early stage of human development, all utterances would be coming from the center as well as the individuals uttering them—even at this "late" stage the distinction cannot be established absolutely—what we say is always, also, coming from elsewhere.) While the recipient of the command might be repeating the entire ostensive-imperative "pair" as an act of deferral (to maintain linguistic presence), for the other, who has now "asked a question," the order given to the object would provide the "answer." In the question and the declarative sentence we now have a new "pair"—indeed, every declarative sentence only makes sense in terms of the question, or questions, we take it to be answering. An "answer" is the prolongation of the question until a possible or hypothetical new ostensive is presented, which places both interlocutors under the authority of an imperative from the center including them in a space with the new world of things.

V

THE CENTER AND THE DECLARATIVE

Social thought has an obligation to maintain linguistic presence, and the way this is done is through a minimal vocabulary distinguishing one mode of thought from another, and sustained consistently so as to generate new concepts. I take Gans's derivation of the successive speech forms to be that minimal vocabulary. Originary thinking relies upon concepts shared with other modes of thought within the human sciences, such as "desire," "resentment," "mimesis," "sign," "representation" and more. I will use these terms and many others—I won't be generating an entirely new theoretical language, just a theoretical center organized around the speech forms and the center to which all utterances must be traced and directed: this theoretical center will control my use of all other terms. Gans, beyond his analysis through *The Origin of Language*, uses the different speech forms to designate different cultural forms—in both *The End of Culture* and *Originary Thinking*, Gans speaks of "ostensive culture," "imperative culture" and 'declarative culture." Moreover, Gans uses the speech forms to mark decisive shifts in high culture: most notably, he defines "metaphysics" as the assumption that the declarative sentence is the primary speech act; and, through a reading of Moses's encounter with God on Mt. Horeb as described in *Exodus*, he identifies the specific innovation of Hebraic monotheism as the "discovery" of the God whose name is a declarative sentence. The burden of this book is to follow those trails and work out a social, political and cultural theory, or, as I will call it, an "anthropomorphics," as an originary grammar of the center. So, I will show that speaking in terms of the imperatives we are conveying, or hearing, from the center, when discussing declarative sentences and discourse, will yield (through refinements in interrogative culture) insights (or, ostensive regions) unavailable when following more conventional imperatives to speak about sentences and discourses in terms of meanings packaged by one mind for others according to specific explicit and tacit rules. Beyond the heuristic value of originary grammar, I will insist on taking it quite literally: there is no way we could ever be doing anything that is not following an imperative within a network of imperatives deriving from an ostensive world and explicated by declaratives. We are semiotic beings, composed of signs and signs ourselves, and the ostensive, imperative, interrogative and declarative are the most elementary signs—equivalent, in a rough way, to Charles Sanders Peirce's icon, index and symbol.[1] All we do is try to follow what the center is telling us to do. Even more, we are of the center, which speaks through us.

To begin to give a sense of the implications of this approach, or imperative, I'm going to take some time to analyze a small part of Andrew Bartlett's groundbreaking originary analysis of science, published in *Anthropoetics* in 2007, "Originary Science, Originary Memory: Frankenstein and the Problem of Modern Science." Here, Bartlett traces the origins of science to the need to find a substitute for the central object on subsequent ritual scenes. The first "knowledge," in this case, is of the appropriateness of another object to function as the object already inscribed in the community's memory has functioned—the question is whether the new object is "similar" or "analogous" enough to that previous object. I will not be exploring Bartlett's argument in any detail, much less try to reproduce its full complexity; I am using it to clarify the implications of an "originary grammar of the center"

---

1 I find that my discussion is lacking the needed inquiry into what we could call "interrogative culture," probably because the interrogative is a special case of the imperative—it's an imperative converted from a demand for an object or action (or non-action) into a request for information. But disciplinary spaces are grounded in cultures of questioning, in which the mark of a good question is that, first, it follows (or is converted from) an ordinarily functional but now failed imperative; and, second, that it generates declaratives that open new ostensive fields that cancel the interrogative while being impossible without it. We could say that interrogatives are a special kind of command: to create new ostensives in place of where ostensives had become absent.

precisely due to its rigorous immersion in and deployment of the conceptual terms of originary thinking:

> One space of tension, as we have seen, is that between the originary "usurper" whose proximity to the *new* possibly-sacred substitute object and to the object itself risks his being victimized by the community (the usurper as metonym of the new object he introduces). The other space of tension is the yes or no of the "analogy" the members of the community may or may not be prepared to draw—relying on originary memory of the image-of-the-object as I have outlined it above—between the new and the original object. Inasmuch as originary memory reproduces a memory of the whole scene and the whole event, all forces tend toward the community's peaceful acceptance of the new object: the usurper wishes to minimize the risk of violence to himself, and the community wishes to minimize the risk to itself. An object as close in "image" as possible to the original object must be the most appropriate object, because an object as close in "image" as possible to the original object would risk the least disassociation between originary event and ritual repetition, between the "image" in originary memory and its possible re-presentation in a new object of economic value. What I contend, however, is that the "conservative" minimalization of the difference between objects is *not a guarantee of the absolute preservation of the sacrality of the original object, but rather a measure of the minimality of originary desacralization: the minimality of "originary science."* That originary science is the sign in the mode of a minimal desacralization is precisely what we should expect. The other imperative, however, is maximal exchangeability: and the new object, to be exchangeable, must be permitted to be different, to have differential significance. Originary science pays intense, almost total respect to religious imperatives. It is no one other than the originary scientific "usurper" who asks the community to exchange this new, "real" object for the old, remembered, now less "real" object, which risks losing some of its sacred power as the necessary consequence of the differential information being created. The *new* object will not be the same object; therefore, it must present a minimal threat to communal solidarity. Therefore, when Gans writes of the original sign being "applied to a referent other than the original one" he includes the notion of a "diminution of intensity" in the sign itself. The scientific, I suggest, has there

with that "diminution" taken a little bit away from the sacred. Nor should we be surprised that the originary meeting of the sacred and profane occurs with the usurper's production of differential information: "This first differentiation would create a two-place hierarchy of signs constitutive of the opposition between sacred and profane representations" (79). The first "profane" representation may be considered the first "scientific" representation.

I want to emphasize that I have no substantive differences with this passage or, indeed, Bartlett's entire analysis (which will be echoed in my own discussion). I simply want to point to a couple of instances of language indicating intentionality that will highlight a critical element of originary method I pointed to before—that in identifying a new cultural form, no semiotic resources that could only have been a product of that form can be part of the hypothesis regarding its creation. So, the "usurper" introducing the new object "risks being victimized," and presumably is aware of, can formulate a representation of, this risk. The community, then, may or may not be prepared to draw an analogy between the original object and its replacement. Finally, and most importantly, the usurper "wishes" to minimize this risk, and the community shares this same "wish."

Bartlett is aware that neither the usurper nor the community has the language to formulate this "wish" or this risk assessment—not too much prior to this passage he discussed the same problem, through a passage of Gans's discussing it, that I addressed above regarding the problem of "speaking for" those on the scene. We have to assume some continuity amidst the discontinuity that enables us to hypothesize usefully—something like what Bartlett describes here must, indeed, be happening. The question is how we represent that. Bartlett here (and, really, only in these fairly unimportant instances) does so by constructing a subject and a field of subjects capable of formulating wishes and carrying out risk assessment. These are subjects, then, with an internal mental space that can subsist "horizontally," that is, in relation to the other subjects in the field, without any reference to the center. Let's remember the problem here: to determine whether the new object is, for the purposes of ritual, the "same" as the original object. So, we imagine the members of the group working it out, with the usurper trying to introduce an object that won't be seen as too different, with the other members not insisting on seeing differences except for when strictly necessary (or, perhaps, refusing to acknowledge identity except for when unavoidable).

Who actually decides, though? In the end, a substitute object will be used—but who determined its acceptability? How would those on the scene represent the decision as having been made? Could any of them "take responsibility" for it, or "credit" another with having made the decision, or playing a special role in making it? If we are going to pursue these questions, we would have to attribute more and more clearly unavailable language to participants on the scene, and make them far richer "characters" than we can imagine them being. The other way of approaching it would be to say that the center decides. In other words, the representational capacities we would have to attribute to the participants we attribute instead to the center. The center, as we can say, is nothing more than the collective or aggregate signifying capacities of the community. But this doesn't mean those capacities could be disaggregated and redistributed to the members of the community—they are only real in their collective and aggregated form. Each member of the community only sees the other members through the center, as suspended by the center. If the object offered by the usurper does not desacralize minimally enough, it is because the center that subsists beyond any particular object, the center that calls for the object, has rejected it. The risk assessment Bartlett speaks of is a waiting to see if the center will accept the new object. How do the members know what the center has "decided"? By reading the other members as signs of the center, the vehicle through which the center conveys *its* "wishes." If some member were to prevent the new object from being placed at the center, he would be doing so "on assignment" from the center—at least if his initiative prevails. Attributing the decision to the center minimizes our own discontinuity with the participants on this hypothetical scene because if this counter-usurper were to provide a reason for the object's unacceptability, this is the only reason he could give—otherwise, we'd have to imagine him representing the results of his risk-assessment and assessing that risk-assessment relative to other ones represented on the scene. Does this mean that the counter-usurper has "really" decided? We might say so, even though he surely wouldn't; but we shouldn't either, because that would require us to posit some space of decision internal to the counter-usurper, something like a "will," which has not been accounted for. What has been accounted for is the constitution of each member of the community as a protector of the center, and therefore as an arm of the center. As members of the community, they have no other "content."[2]

The problem of determining whether the new object is, ritually, the "same," is the problem of maintaining linguistic presence, with which we are already familiar. It is the problem of determining whether the sign issued in one case is the "same" as that sign issued on a prior occasion. This problem arises already on the originary scene, where each participant must conform his gesture to that of the others, and determine whether the others are doing the same. As in Bartlett's example, there is certainly an allowable margin of error here determined, not by some "objective" assessment in accord with an external "standard," but by whether the sign comes with a body positioned so as to preserve or disrupt the state of suspended animation before the central object. The only way of determining sameness is by seeing whether the center is repelling the others as it is holding oneself in place—which means that the issuance of the sign is itself a following of the "rule" of the center. In each case, what we can reconstruct as a risk assessment is one member detecting a slackening in another's adherence to the rule of the center, and subsequently stepping in, as minimally as possible, as maximally as necessary, to take up that slackening. The center has decided once the slackening has been tightened.

It is the center, first of all, that has agency—human agency will later come to be modeled on the agency of the center. The center issues signs to those on the margin, who in turn convey those signs to one another in collaborations and deliberations that pro-

---

2 I will here direct the reader's attention to another essay of Bartlett's, "From First Hesitation to Scenic Imagination: Originary Thinking with Eric Gans," published in the Girardian journal *Contagion* in 2009. It brilliantly and far more comprehensively covers the theoretical territory of Gans's work up until that point. It's fair to say that I'm defining what I am calling "anthropomorphics" against Bartlett's articulation of Generative Anthropology—and that Bartlett's is far more consistent with Gans's own understanding than is my own. See also his *Mad Scientist, Impossible Human: An Essay in Generative Anthropology.*

duce signs issued back to the center. To take Bartlett's discussion in a different direction, the substitution of successive objects for the originary one transforms the ritual scene from an ostensive one, in which the deity is immediately present, to an imperative one, where the ritual aims at making the deity appear, first of all within the ritual itself but also by providing for the community. But addressing the deity imperatively must itself be done in prescribed forms—that is, pursuant to imperatives issued by the deity itself. The deity, or the center, does not always respond identically to each request made of it. Since the form of the request has been prescribed by the center, these differences must be attributed to differences in the form of the request in each case. Even if the ritual has been carried out, to all appearances, in exactly the same way, something about its performance must be different. From the standpoint of more advanced forms of culture we could say, for example, that the "intent" behind the performance was different in some way (it was only carried out "mechanically," for example). But what we are examining now will provide us with a hypothesis regarding that very difference between performance and intent. No record could have been kept of these early rituals so, even if all a great deal of effort was invested in ensuring the conformity of all to inherited ritual forms, it would always be possible for some member to introduce some innovation as a recovery of the "same," originally effective form. What emerges within this imperative culture is a continual attempt to reduce the difference between performance and effect. This becomes a focus of the community because the "promise" made by the center (to comply with imperatives carried out according to prescription) will not always be "fulfilled," and the only "explanation" for such unfulfilled promises can be some inadequacy in the performance of the ritual. All the words I have been putting in scare quotes ("promise," "fulfill," "explanation") are the products of declaratives constructed so as to confirm that the ritual order remains intact ("the same").

It is in the failure of the imperative that the declarative is born. The ritual scene I am hypothesizing now presupposes the existence of fully developed, that is, declarative language. Following the assumptions laid out earlier regarding the marginal, mistaken nature of new linguistic-cultural forms, we can also assume that both the imperative and the declarative come later to the central scene of ritual. As applied to ritual, the declarative constructs scenes enacting the dialectic of imperatives to and from the center. The community oscillates between successful and unsuccessful ritual performances; the center oscillates between honoring and refusing the requests of the community. If the central being must be called to present itself on the ritual scene, it must be elsewhere and must come from elsewhere. Sometimes it comes, sometimes it doesn't—either something prevents it from coming, or it doesn't want to come. If something prevents it from coming, there are other beings at play—we can see the scenic construction of the center. Sometimes the central being can overcome the obstacles placed in its way; sometimes it can't. If the central being doesn't want to come, it may be because the community has displeased it in some way; or it may be because the central being has other priorities, problems and pleasures of its own to attend to. We can see how the kind of intentional language I wished removed from accounts of interactions between the community and the center have now entered into the discussion—the central being "wants" to come, "overcomes" obstacles, can be "displeased," pursues its own interests and pleasures, and so on. All of this results from the "interpretation" of ritual in declarative terms; or, more precisely, the interpretation of variable results of the imperatives exchanged with the center in declarative terms. These "explanations" of the results of ritual performances are the origins of myth, as a declarative overlay on the imperative structure of ritual. While we can't hypothesize with any great specificity, the origin of words like "want," "wish," "try," "choose," "decide," "like" and "dislike," that is, the whole linguistic apparatus of intentionality, is best considered as emerging to fill gaps between the obedience to the imperatives of the center in ritual scenes and the reciprocal honoring of requests by the center. But these are gaps to be filled in describing activities at the center, and only secondarily to those on the margins. Activities between members of the community are modeled on and arranged by activities at the center, which are far richer in dramatic content and motivation than anything going on at the margin. The human is modeled on the non-human center—this is why I call the human science I am presenting here an "anthropomorphics." Humans anthropomorphized themselves before they could carry out this operation on anything else. And we are still doing so today, as we can remember insofar as we listen to the center.[3]

3   I have been working here, in particular, with Gans's analysis of imperative culture and declarative culture in *The End of Culture*, 112-122.

VI

THE CENTRALITY
OF THE CENTER

What is a center? Whatever can invoke and be referenced by an ostensive sign: the center is both cause and product of the sign—as cause it subsists beyond any particular reference, and as product it is continually renewed. Invoking the sign exceeds the reference, though—it is already the beginning of an imperative. So, a center is a locus of imperative exchange—whatever about the object commands the issuance of the ostensive sign is also an agency of which requests can be made. Under the concept of "imperative exchange" we can include all of our expectations about how the world and others "should" treat us in exchange for what we imagine ourselves to have contributed to the world and others. But it is mimetic desire, and the rivalry and crisis it causes, that leads to the emission of the sign; true, and our ability to pare down language derived from scenes at the center and apply it to proto-human acts that created the center is itself a sign of our current relation to the center. The center is whatever we can compose declaratives about so as to formalize the incommensurabilities between what we ask of the center considered, let's say, as a "situation" or emergent event, and what that center, that situation, that event, yields "in return." We have to start within a fully developed declarative culture in order to reconstruct the emergence of that culture out of its prerequisites. This assumes we have a fully developed vocabulary with carefully refined concepts that have been fully anthropomorphized, and made available for reference to proto-humans and then humans in their "barest," hypothetically minimal state. I will now start examining how that could have become possible.

The center requires defenders, interpreters, collaborators. This includes everyone in the community, but not everyone equally, certainly not in every case. On the originary scene itself it is unimaginable that all members of the group issued the gesture of aborted appropriation at the same time, with the same clarity, with the same effect on other members of the group. This is unimaginable not only because it's extremely unlikely, but because to imagine it would suggest some shared instinctual response, thereby blurring the singularity of the scene itself as the birth of the human. We make it a rule not to overload our hypotheses, but keeping in mind our hypothesis that cultural innovation starts on the mistaken margin and is then aligned with the center, we can assume the initial gesture must have been put forth by a member not too central but also not too marginal. Not too central, that is, not the Alpha of the group, because he has presumably been neutralized from the start and any gesture of hesitation would be one reflecting being overwhelmed rather than symmetrical with others nearby approaching the object. Not too marginal, because we have to imagine the gesture being issued by someone who might be a threat, if it is to be noticed and imitated. We assume minimal awareness of what is being done—rather than projecting the entire scene, its possible consequences, and the "hope" of reversing those consequences (awareness that could only be retrojected back into the scene much later through a narrative consciousness) back into the first signer, we can assume one member proceeding step by step towards the center with his fellows, somewhat unevenly, falling a little behind, seeing their attention drawn to his slowdown, and accentuating that slowdown through posture and gesture only slightly but noticeably different than that of the others. The more they notice, the more he accentuates; the more they accentuate the more the convergence toward the center rears back and goes into reverse. The scene will be successful when there are enough who have exchanged the sign to restrain those who have not yet caught on—at this point, those who have been rehearsing the sign are acting on behalf of the center, as they attend from the central object to its imminent violators, and back again.

Differences in proximity to the center proliferate even in the most egalitarian communities. Indeed, egalitarianism is merely fractal hierarchy: unless we imagine genuinely spontaneous collective action, in any instance someone goes first and shapes the field for the others. The only purpose of imagining such spontaneous collectivity is to erase the firstness and minimize the resentments resulting from the fear that the one first on the scene might try to extend that firstness beyond the scene it constitutes. Defending firstness in order to allow the field to be shaped is done in the name of the center; restricting firstness so as to allow new fields to be shaped is also done in the name of the center. Erasing firstness altogether is itself a bid for the center, in the name of repressing all "illegitimate" bids. Fractal hierarchy means that the hierarchy assumed in some distribution of shared attention organized into intention will position the agents in such a way as to generate new hierarchies. These turnovers can be rapid; they can be indefinitely delayed—there can be no "rules" about this (even if there are explicit rules, those rules need to be enforced, and someone would have to take the lead in doing that, thereby generating more fractal hierarchy). Someone who has set the field once will be more likely to take and be given the opportunity to do so again; all the more, someone who has done so 2, 3, 5, 20 times. Here we can see the origin of power, not in the exercise of force and violence over others in the community; rather, the origin of power lies with the continuation of the deferral exercised on the originary scene, in this case by someone who is willing to take more risks, accept more suffering and deprivation in the course of accomplishing some task and, most importantly, stand both inside the scene and outside of it so as to modulate the desires and resentments of others who need to be brought into the scene. This modulation is carried out ostensively, through naming everyone else on the scene, even if this naming simply involves assigning positions (the one who does this as well as the one who is this).

I am drawing on anthropology and history but I am not writing anthropology or history: "anthropomorphics" is completely hypothetical, following the originary hypothesis itself. All thinking is hypothetical, insofar as the issuance of any sign hypothesizes regarding the way the sign will "magnetize" a given field. I have been leading up to the emergence of permanent social hierarchies, and I mention these methodological considerations here to help make this discussion and, as much as possible, other discussions of social hierarchies, a source of deferral rather than resentment.

Among those members of the community who establish the most lasting positions of leadership, each of them acting in the name of the center, one of them will eventually seize and occupy the (at this point still) ritual center. The term within anthropology for this position is the "Big Man."[1] Leadership through deferral is acquired by accumulation and distribution to one's dependents, and through the gift economy with one's peers and rivals. If one leader can throw a big enough potlatch to bankrupt his rivals and turn them all into dependents, then he has occupied the center, not only sacralizing himself but making himself the source of social distribution. There are, of course, millennia across which the historical transformations of the Big Man into sacral kingship—and then into divine kingship—extend,[2] along with the myriad forms taken by each of these political arrangements, and correspondingly diverse forms of priesthood paralleling them. I am only going to be interested in all of these in terms of the strict concerns of anthropomorphics, or the originary grammar of the center.

1 Gans first discusses the "Big Man" (a concept originally developed by Marshall Sahlins) in *The End of Culture*, 150-162.
2 My discussion of these institutions will be heavily indebted to Marshall Sahlins and David Graeber's *On Kings*.

VII

THE GENERATIVITY
OF THE CENTER

I mentioned earlier that in the earliest communities, the center is far more "dramatic," which is also to say, far more "human," than the actual human margin. As David Graeber points out, it is not, strictly speaking, correct to refer to these early, formally egalitarian communities as "non-hierarchical." Quite to the contrary, they are subjected to the most asymmetrical and arbitrary hierarchies as they are ruled by the mythical occupants of the center. The very earliest occupants of the center would be the transfigured forms of the animals placed at the center for ritual purposes and consumption. These beings are the progenitors, guardians, and nemeses of the community. Until the ritual center is rendered non-figural, we can assume all worship is ancestor worship, very much including animals, because the center has generated the community. The more differentiation there is regarding proximity to the center, the more humans would be so transfigured and take their place in the pantheon of worship. Remembered ancestors founding and continuing specific family and communal lines become figures of worship. It also follows that the more humans can be elevated among those who have given themselves for the continuance and provision of the community, the more they can be ritually placed in that position. Eventually, some individual seizes the ritual and distributive center: this first adventurer or usurper is the "Big Man" widely noted in anthropological accounts. The apotheosis of this development is sacral kingship,[1] in which the

---

1 Here I am indebted to Francis Oakley's *Kingship: The Politics of Enchantment.*

king, as mediator between the community and the cosmos, serves as both power center and ritual center. Needless to say, the configurations vary widely, but the sacral king, I am assuming, is the first object of scapegoating and human sacrifice. Failures of the community are failures to match otherworldly configurations, to do on earth as is done in heaven, and for this the king bears complete responsibility. The unity of paradoxical, signifying center and the central figure first evident on the originary scene remains intact in sacral kingship, which no doubt accounts for the pervasiveness and longevity of this social form, and even in the extension of its ramifications into modern political leadership.

A pure form of sacral kingship would entail the election of an individual who compels that election by his deferral capacities, which provide proof that sacral agencies look favorably upon him; and the killing and subsequent mythical transfiguration of that individual as soon as those agencies gave signs of withholding their favor. When whatever "credit" the king has accumulated has been exhausted would have to be determined by those close enough to the signifying center to "read" those signs. We can assume some alliance between prospective rivals and priests in charge of the rituals, if there are such separate from the king himself. Some degree of what would look to us like cynicism would be involved in such transfers of divine favor: the failure of the king to lead a successful campaign, or some waste of resources would be "interpreted" in terms of some ritual violation of a sacred injunction. But there's no need to assume that anything like cynicism is even possible here, because that would assume there is some other vocabulary in which "rational assessments" of the performance of the king could be made, and in which a "strategy" for deploying the merely "ideological" ritual and mythical language could be plotted out. Only once the center has been "unfigured" and its human occupant shorn of sacrality could such a vocabulary emerge. Decisions that would be intelligible to external perspectives would be made, because the ritual and mythical vocabulary in which thinking takes place allows them to be made—which is not to say the rationality will be quite the same as that of the retroactive observer, who would be required to reconstruct the relation to the center constitutive of events in that community.

Approximations to this "pure" form of sacral kingship could

certainly endure, but the form would be a continual source of rivalry that would, at least in some cases, lead to the ritualization of the selection and transference of kingly power. This would formalize kingship and the deferral capacities of the community. The individual who most displays the power of deferral would not thereby be elevated to the center—a process of establishing and choosing from among candidates would be put in place. Nor is the king removed immediately when those deferral powers are seen to wane—scheduled transfers of power, among them perhaps the sacrifice of the king, or explicit rules or agents that must be followed or consulted are established. This increases the permanence of the occupation of the center—if the earned leadership that characterizes the Big Man and the model of "pure" sacral kingship I posited above is no longer the means by which power is assumed, the mechanisms and lessons of previous efforts at ruling can be collected, canonized, and provided pedagogically to the future ruler who would now have time to prepare to take his position. At this point some diremption between state ritual and more localized rituals would take place: the king is still the father of the people, who controls and distributes the resources of the community, and to whom sacrifices must therefore be brought, but his protection and therefore distance from the most active resentments and rivalries within the community make him a less effective mediator; such mediation would therefore be relocated within familial cults. This is the point of transition from sacral kingship to the divine kingship that characterized the gigantic empires of the ancient world.

Once a human has occupied the center, the possibility has opened for any human to become a center. I am going to provide an account of how that possibility has been actualized, but to do so it will help to explain what it means for anyone capable of issuing an utterance to be a center. To be a center means that attention can be made to converge upon it in such a way that it can be seen to be caused by representations coming from that center. Convergent attention is a source of rivalry and possible hostility: if your presence and self-representation becomes a source of rivalry, it can be posited as a cause of that rivalry, and your removal from the game in some way thereby a means of eliminating the danger raised by that rivalry. Your self-representations can also become a source of deferral—indeed, it is most likely that one becomes a source of deferral through the management of rivalries generated by oneself as a desirable object. One can obviously be desirable and therefore a cause of rivalry in any number of ways, depending upon where one is positioned within the mimetic field. And there are, equally obviously, innumerable ways of converting rivalry and resentment deriving from one's presence into deferral and love. How one operates as a self or individual depends upon how one exercises self-representation as a center so as to favor some possibilities over others; insofar as one becomes less "functional" as an individual, that would indicate that the center is not holding, perhaps because of a failure to attract sufficient convergent attention to acquire the means to construct oneself as a source of deferral; perhaps due to an excess of convergent attention (which can be addictive), overwhelming efforts to become a site of deferral. If we were to develop an "originary psychology," this would be the starting point. This is the way in which what Gans calls "omnicentrism,"[2] or what I would call "the generalization of anthropomorphization," proceeds.

To put this another way, to be a center is to be subject to attempts at appropriation and ostensive gestures: one can be appropriated bodily, for example, sexually; one can be appropriated as model; one can be appropriated as a proxy; and so on. Appropriation, for humans, is mediated by ostensive signs indicating deferral and the acknowledgment of other appropriative claims, including those of the one being appropriated. The relation between the appropriation and the gesture, on the one hand, and the degree of reciprocity between the one being appropriated and the one appropriating, can vary from violent appropriation with a minimal attribution of consent to the victim, on one extreme, to publicly recognized, ceremonial pledges of fidelity and respect, on the other. To be a center, further, is to give and receive imperatives—not just explicit requests, commands, demands, pleas, and so on, but the imperatives one gives off merely as a publicly recognized center: imperatives to keep a certain distance, to approach only in certain culturally acceptable ways (but also to, nevertheless, approach), and to look to yourself and your own self-construction as a center. We give off such imperatives through our speech,

2 See Gans's *Originary Thinking*, 219.

dress, manners, posture, choice of location, and so on, and they are constructed in dialogue with the imperatives given off by others. Finally, to be a center is to be a source of declaratives: statements and narratives representing discrepancies between the various imperatives one gives off, between the imperatives one gives off and those that one obeys, and between the imperatives one gives off and those others located "similarly" give off: the problem is always to say how can one be the same as others in being a center, given all the differences in this particular way of self-centering.

Divine kingship involves conquest and the control of vast territories and therefore makes it possible to treat populations as means—in particular, human sacrifice and slavery. The king, whether divine himself or not, is sanctioned divinely, while masses of people are treated as nameless within the system of naming. Under sacral kingship, everyone in the community shares the same ritual order—everyone is named by the center. That is no longer the case. The other notable breach in the order of sacral kingship is the emergence of populations extrinsic to the order, even if produced by that order—such as younger sons without inheritance, and hence any access to the family hearth, in systems with primogeniture. It would be the more successful, imminently if not actually imperial, sacral kingships that would generate the most "anomalies" in relation to the ritual order. In this sense, these sacral kingships converge with divine kingships while also, most notably in the case of the ancient Greek city-states, entering into competition and conflict with them. Once there are groups, or a "people," outside of the ritual order, kingly rule itself steps outside of that ritual order to maintain and strengthen itself. To be outside of the ritual order is to have no social existence, which is, first of all, to be merely a means, whether for productive or political purposes; it is, secondly, to be defined solely in terms of opposition to the ritual order, to specific groups within the ritual order (who are now also defined oppositionally), and to other groups outside of that order. Struggles amongst kings, aristocrats and "the people" only make sense once a breach has opened up in the inclusive ritual order. The origin of the "tyrant," as a political concept, lies in this breach—the tyrant is simply a king who is not sanctified as the occupant of the ritual center, but defined by his rule through the manipulation of conflicts between social groups.[3] The "tyrant" is the central problem the foundation of political thought aims to solve, and it remains the problem political thought has yet to solve. This is because "tyranny" is an unsolvable problem without the creation of a social order grounded in the imperatives issued by an originary center—and such an order cannot be grasped by political thinking derived from the problem of the tyrant.

With the breach of the order of sacral kingship we find money and markets established by kings and used by them as political instruments. David Graeber[4] notes that markets are established, and money provided to make those markets functional, for the purpose of provisioning soldiers stationed in foreign territories. Richard Seaford[5] points out that in Ancient Greece money was provided by the king to purchase animals for cultic sacrifices. Markets represent forms of delegation by the central authority—markets are areas of social life that are not under direct sovereign supervision. Any form of supervision generates margins where supervision lapses—markets are established when these margins need to be formalized and supervised indirectly. Money is a means of subordinating market activity to central authority—that is, money is a form taken by the delegation of power, and is therefore a form of power itself. Money is the power to command the labor of others. The pluralization of power within the polity means that power centers can align themselves with or against the king, and the king can align himself with some power centers against others. With money, markets and plural power centers comes justice systems, secular thought and at least the beginnings of technology. Justice systems because adjudication of disputes between relatively equal power centers requires rules and judges to apply and enforce those rules; secular thought, because thinking in terms of "Nature," or some equivalent, is the only way to try and name figures and practices outside of the ritual order;[6] and technology, because once humans are objects, levied *en masse* in slave gangs, as soldiers, or reduced by debt to landless laborers, it becomes possible to think of the use of tools and the analysis

3   I am relying on Fustel de Coulanges's *The Ancient City* here.
4   In *Debt: The First 5,000 Years.*
5   *Money and the Early Greek Mind: Homer, Philosophy, Tragedy*
6   Seaford also points, in a very interesting and powerful way, to the ways in which money as a universalizing equivalent makes abstract thought possible.

and articulation of objects outside of ritual constraints.

VIII

METALANGUAGE AND
METAPOLITICS

With concepts like "nature" and "justice," it becomes possible to model social relations on desacralized terms, in accord with the reduction of these and related concepts to their most minimal meaning in opposition to the sacred order and "arbitrary" tyranny alike. Essences can be attributed to different social groups and classes, along with deviations from those essences: conformity with the essence equals nature, and relating to individuals, and constructing relations between groups, according to nature, is justice. "Materialism," "the spirit of domination," and "greed" are among the forms taken by those deviations, as power centers can be imagined and, no doubt, seen, acting at large in accord with roles they are given within markets and politics. Tyranny is the manifestation of and response to greed and the desire for domination, "passions" liberated on the post-sacral market. Greed and power hunger can be identified by those who have liberated themselves from it, by establishing justice within themselves and restoring themselves to nature. The post-priestly class of philosophers makes a bid to become a new source of power by presenting itself as in command of the concepts that make ruling "legitimate," that is, non-tyrannical: nature and justice. The power of the philosopher, his access to what might be called *imperium in imperio*, but which I would prefer to call the "super-sovereignty" inherent in the proper understandings of the conceptual criteria to which sovereignty must yield so as to be non-tyrannical, itself relies upon the spread of writing. Writing is also a product of divine kingship and markets, originating in the recording of transactions and eventually becoming a means of recording and reconstructing language so as to make it visible to central authority.

As I mentioned earlier, Eric Gans locates the origin of the two leading streams of Western culture, Ancient Greece and Ancient Israel, in terms of the prioritizing of the declarative sentence. In the case of the Greeks, the founding of metaphysics involves treating the declarative sentence, the proposition, as the primary linguistic form—in direct opposition to the ritual, sacrificial ostensive and the imperatives it unfolds.[1] In the case of Israel, we have a new kind of God, who cannot be invoked imperatively—cannot be the other side of an imperative exchange—because his name is a declarative sentence.[2] In both cases, this isolation and elevation of the declarative sentence is possible only in scribal and comparatively literate cultures. In discussing metaphysics' hypostatization of the declarative sentence, I will draw upon David Olson's studies of the cognitive consequences of literacy, in particular his classic *The World on Paper: The Conceptual and Cognitive Implications of Writing and Reading* and his recent work, *The Mind on Paper: Reading, Consciousness and Rationality*. The use of writing to represent speech, according to Olson, constitutes language as an object of inquiry: the determination of how to use marks on a surface to represent spoken words is that inquiry, constructing such things as "phonemes," "words" and "sentences" as theoretical objects. The very possibility of asking what a word means, what it "really" means, as is often one of the opening moves of the Socratic dialogue, presupposes that "words" have already been identified as separate from each other and given "official" meanings through the written text, just as the construction of a logic is merely an elaboration of various possibilities allowable given the possibility of defining words and a grammatical structure that could only have been fixed through writing. The "picture" of language that comes "naturally" to us as literate people, and that has dominated modern pedagogy is a direct result of the mode of inquiry into language undertaken in order to represent speech: for the most part, and especially when we're not thinking about it too much, we see language as comprised of a huge collection of individual words with circumscribed meanings which can be combined in

---

1   See Gans's "Plato and the Birth of Conceptual Thought."
2   Gans, *Science and Faith*, especially Chapter 3, "The Mosaic Revelation," 51-88.

infinite ways in accord with grammatical rules. A much more accurate representation of language would be as a finite, if immense, web of utterances all of which are variations of previous utterances ultimately descended from an originary scene, organized through a hierarchy of core utterances which have become virtual templates and sources of more differentiated utterances. In the former case, we see each other, as linguistic beings, as depositories of abstracted "content" and rules of combination which we are obliged to obey; in the latter case, we see each other as generative modelers, always varying and expanding the field of possible utterances.

The speech scene is comprised of features that cannot be directly represented in writing, features involving the physical presences of the participants on the scene, such as tone, inflection, gesture and posture, the proximity of speakers to each other and so on. The writing systems we know of did not attempt to directly represent those features of the speech scene. Instead, the development of writing involved the creation of a meta-language used to represent indirectly those features of the speech scene. Olson has us imagine a written text as the reporting of a speech act. Now, in the reporting of another's speech act in person, the speech act can be acted out as a whole—the tone and inflections can be imitated, the postures and gestures can be acted out, and even commentary on the speech being reported can be enacted through approving or dismissive facial expressions and otherwise. Writing, then, has to supplement all the elements of this performance that it can't directly represent. This is what the metalanguage of literacy does. To perform another's speech act, you would only, strictly speaking, need the word "say" and perhaps one or two other words to refer to what the speaker has said. If you need to supplement that report with all the other elements of the speech scene, you need a whole phalanx of other words, words which provide information regarding those other elements: "stated," "suggested," "assumed," "implied," "considered," "criticized," and so on. Olson further points out that through the nominalization of these verbs we generate the material for a vast disciplinary order, in which we study "assumptions," "statements," "implications," "criticism" and much more.[3] In hypostatizing the declarative sentence, metaphys-

3 See *The World on Paper*, chapters 4 and 5, 65-114.

ics merely treats the metalanguage of literacy as referring to an actual, if ideal, order.

The telos of writing, according to Olson's more recent argument,[4] is to construct a scene upon which the writer and reader both stand. Drawing upon Frances Noel-Thomas and Mark Turner's study of what they call "classic prose" in their *Clear and Simple as the Truth: Writing Classic Prose*, Olson sees writing as seeking to efface itself before a simulated scene. This requires the abolition of any ostensive dimension to the written text—that is, anything that draws attention to the text as written, to the scene of writing, the scene of reading, and the scene represented in the writing as being distinct scenes that must be articulated, ultimately by the reader. It presupposes a private reader, alone with the text, in a kind of silent conversation with the author as opposed, say, to a public or group reading, or reading that serves the purpose of memorizing ritual formulas and myths. The consequence of metaphysics, then, is what Gans calls an "internal scene of representation,"[5] where one constitutes oneself as a center of one's own attention, as one observes oneself alone with the world of ideas made up of the metalanguage of literacy. This is one way the broaching of the sacral order plays out, as this internal scene of representation can only be represented and maintained in opposition to everything that would define the individual as something other than an internalized private order—in opposition to both any ritual order and any social claims. This is a mythicized subject, entitled to be permitted to act in accord with spontaneously emerging and self-ordered "assumptions," "conclusions," "beliefs," and so on; in fact, functioning as a proxy for the post-metaphysi-

4 *The Mind on Paper*, Chapter 2, "Inventing Writing: The History of Writing and the Ontogeny of Writing," 19-38.
5 I have been unable to determine where, exactly, Gans first uses the concept, but this, from a recent *Chronicle of Love and Resentment* (#577, February 24, 2018), is a fairly representative usage: "The esthetic cannot be understood without postulating an internal scene of representation on which the recipient of a sign, formal or institutional, or a worldly perception experienced as significant, 'imagines' the referent of the sign." As is perhaps evident from Gans's assertion of the indispensability of the concept, my usage differs significantly from his own. Gans sees the internal scene of representation as a product of the originary scene (even if that's not stated explicitly here) and therefore as constitutively human, whereas I see it as a product of desacralization and the abstraction of the declarative order from the ostensive-imperative world.

cal disciplines which deploy the metalanguage of literacy in power plays on the field of super-sovereignty.

Hebrew scripture, and then the Christian Testament, represent a different trajectory of the "promoted" declarative sentence. Metaphysics aims at abstracting declarative culture from the ostensive-imperative world as completely as possible—metaphysics never comes to an end because this abstraction can never be complete: the world can never be completely described through declarative sentences that are comprised of words that can themselves be defined in declarative sentences without ever having to come to rest upon an ostensively defined word—ultimately, a name. Scripture maintains continuity with the sacred order by treating the declarative sentence as an inquiry into the ostensive-imperative world—as I put it earlier, as an inquiry into the discrepancies evident in imperative exchanges. It does this by singling out, in newly declarative terms, the victim produced ostensively in sacrificial orders. Once we have, with a monetized, indebted, marketized, politically plural world, justice systems, victims are officially recognized within those systems. Rather than relying upon mimetic contagion or the ritually prescribed selection of victims, new means must be created for determining what counts as victimization. New concepts of intentionality and consequence are constructed, ultimately out of the metalanguage of literacy. So, far, nothing in these new arrangements upsets the order of divine kingship, or the imperial order: sacrifice can continue as usual, while relatively minor disputes get settled in increasingly sophisticated ways.

But with the justice system comes the possibility of being a victim, not just of another player within the system, but of the system, and its head, and its entire conceptual order. There would be losers within the justice system who would refuse to accept their loss. Usually, these refusals would be attempts to revert to some kind of honor, or vendetta system, in which offenses are repaid in kind by those who have authority over the victim. Such futile resistance to the imperial order would be easily suppressed, but would nevertheless mark the system as productive of victims who are heroic on still recognizable terms. It thereby becomes possible to represent the refusal to accept official judgment outside of the domain and discipline of judgment itself, to some broader public or audience. In that case, one would simply be representing oneself as a victim and inviting others to see themselves as victims in "analogous" ways, while itemizing the predations of the imperial order upon one of its loyal, perhaps even privileged, subjects, who appealed to it in good faith. Such action would draw upon itself the concentrated wrath of the imperial center, probably in stages, making it possible to represent the unfolding of that wrath and display it against a larger pattern of systematic dispossession, which now becomes visible in a new way by "analogy" to this "injustice." The social death to be suffered by the victim would itself be analogized to the social death experienced, and now newly named, by the massive slave classes of the imperial order. This new kind of victim, drawing upon himself a new form of collective attention, would be or represent a new kind of divinity.

I put all this forward as a hypothesis regarding the conditions of possibility of the new way of representing the victim in Hebrew and then Christian scripture. Clearly, the "story" I have just told could approximate various skeletal narratives that would themselves represent layers of retelling and revision of some perhaps rather different sequence of events. To construct such stories that place the victim of imperial violence where the hero would have been in sacral narratives would require systematic, deliberate revisions of myth. To organize narratives around the victim of false and violent sacrally grounded imperial orders, as opposed to around the founders of such orders, or those rightly (if "tragically") punished for violating them, would require a volume of substitutions of vocabulary and syntactical orders that could only be carried out under scribal conditions, where the declarative sentence can be isolated, and preserving the text can itself become a divine command around which gather various oral traditions. Such "scriptural" orders are intrinsically anti-imperial because they posit, precisely in order to oppose and discredit the entire imperial order, an imperial order that includes and transcends all other imperial orders: God's empire, to which His people can be directly subject. This is why the opening of Hebrew scripture systematically, if compactly and implicitly, revises and resets the mythological orders underpinning the surrounding empires; it is also why the law recorded in the Pentateuch, as noted by Joshua Berman in his *Created Equal: How the Bible Broke with Ancient*

Political Thought, is egalitarian in a very thoroughgoing way in the precise sense of subordinating each Israelite directly to God, bypassing any other imperial allegiance, but in a way modeled on the covenants between vassal and imperial states. Everyone in such an order is equal in the sense that everyone must be made a site of resistance to subjugation to the sacral imperial order. The subsequent narrative of Hebrew scripture, though, represents the failure to sustain this covenantal structure, leaving us in a position consistent with the working out of metaphysics: the empire of God is reduced to the compass of the internal scene of representation, in the form of a "conscience" that also invokes a super-sovereignty by which the central authority is to be exposed, and to which it must submit—if not now, then perhaps much later. The tendency here is to pit, in a kind of absolute opposition, the center within the center against a world of tyrants.

IX

POST-SACRIFICIAL CENTRALITY

You can say the king should rule because someone must occupy the center, and the occupation of the center relies upon unanimous attention involving the suspension of resentment toward the center; and that the king occupies the center according to traditions and practices predicated on the exclusion of the rivalries expected to emerge once the transition to a new king is necessary, and that preserving these traditions and practices is more important than any preference any of us might have for one candidate over another. Here, rule and sacrality are one. But the identity of rule and sacrality cannot be maintained, because the divine king must be identified with the origin of the community, meaning that such an order rests upon human sacrifice. This is the trajectory of imperative exchange: the more the ruler stands in for the community, the more his life must be hostage to the community's fortunes; the more the ruler is the source of all benefits, the more nothing less than human life can be given in exchange for such largesse. Metaphysics and scripture, each in its own way, exposes and prohibits human sacrifice or scapegoating, or, more broadly, what we can call "violent centralizing." In Gans's account of the transition of the Mosaic to the Christian revelation in *Science and Faith*, he develops the Girardian critique of scapegoating as embodied in the figure of Jesus. Once God is inaccessible through ritualized imperative exchange, we can only obey God in our treatment of fellow humans. The figure—the prophets of Hebrew scripture and then, most inclusively, Jesus—who insistently points out that God can't possibly want all of the sacrifices offered to

Him himself becomes the center of convergent and violent attention on the part of the community. The injunction that we all treat each "as we would wish to be treated," or, we could say, as he or she who is not to be sacrificed, in essence accuses the rest of the community of doing (or at least desiring) precisely that, and the sacrifice or scapegoating of the "messenger" amply confirms that denunciation. This deifies the persecuted one, who has exposed, in the most practical and memorable way possible, the baselessness of our sacrificial practices, which serve only to avoid our terror of indistinction or mimetic crisis.

This is what creates the possibility for each and every one of us to become a center—that is, as one who is not to be sacrificed or violently centralized. We owe the God who has revealed this to us everything, which is to say all that makes up our own centrality. The only possible repayment of this debt is to defer violent centralization wherever one sees it, including placing yourself between the violent mob and the victim. This is an intellectual or cognitive problem as much as it is a moral one—the two, in fact, cannot be separated. We can, perhaps, all recognize a violent mob when it is just about to descend upon its victim. It is more difficult, though, to identify that which, in the discourse of a potential mob, is marking the victim, perhaps in a preliminary way. Even harder is to trace the origins of violent centralizing further back to institutions that license, perhaps implicitly and unknowingly, the onset of mob-inducing discourses. Perhaps even harder than all this is to determine what would counter, expose or reform such institutions and practices. Once the sacrificial order has been exposed, people can devote their lives to answering these questions. The God to which we devote ourselves by pursuing these questions is clearly not one who can be embodied in a specific ruler. The ultimate failure of Christendom to establish the divine sanction of kings is evidence of this. It's therefore easy to follow a line of thought that leads, ultimately, to modern liberalism and democracy, which seem to institutionalize the sanctity of the individual that germinated throughout the development of the medieval Christian order.

It's also easy to see, though, that nothing has replaced, with any unanimity, the sacred aura of kingship. We can see modern politics as a series of replacements for that sacral legitimation, from "freedom" to "the people," to "individual rights," to the "nation," some oppressed class or group, and so on. These terms are the source of endless arguments because they are in themselves nothing more than signs of resentment towards some previous form of sacralized empire, now marked as "tyranny." If you ask someone what "equality" means, you will inevitably be told that it means someone can't take something from you—the concept itself has no substance. It merely marks a presumably inviolable center to be protected from tyranny. Moreover, these modern forms of legitimation have never corresponded particularly well to actual social relations, which remain every bit as hierarchical and, in most areas of life, "dictatorial" as most historical "tyrannies." Demands for more democracy or equality are demands that the state act on your behalf against some of your enemies; it thereby empowers the state, and whichever agencies are best able to access and leverage the state. It follows, further, that the way for the more powerful players in the modern world—state agencies and corporate leaders alike—to enhance their power is precisely by leveraging such concepts against their rivals. Indeed, we can see that "equality" can't really mean anything more than the same in relation to central power, and that for central power to treat everyone the same it must acquire ever more power over all of them. So, we see in the modern world, in democracy and liberalism, not the continuation of the repudiation of sacrifice enacted in metaphysics and (more completely) in scripture, but its revival, as violent centralizing is "laundered" through the institutions that, in purporting to balance powers against each other, actually unleashes them against each other. There will never be an end to finding new forms of tyranny being exercised over one's own inexpressible centrality; indeed, one's own inner self can be the internalization of such tyrannies, through the "colonization" of the mind. The means of self-centering are distributed to all of us equipped with various devices (we might say "apps") for leveraging, mobilizing and activating those means to wind us up as proxies for various liberalizing raids.[1]

---

1 This discussion can be taken as an anthropomorphic reading of Chris Bond's *Nemesis*; see also my "Power and Paradox."

X

SIGNIFYING CENTER,
OCCUPIED CENTER

Once the central object has been distributed, or has distributed itself, and been consumed, the scene itself may be reassembled on another occasion. Something remains beyond the distribution and consumption. Whatever that is, whatever, we might say, has inscribed itself in the practices of the community, is the signifying center. The central problem of history, once the center has been occupied but sacral kingship no longer articulates an occupying and signifying center, is to ensure consistency between these two modes of centrality. Such consistency depends upon contributions from the margins to the center. The center distributes by issuing commands, and the command obeyed has to be the same as the command issued. It is made the same by the contribution of the subject to converting the gap between command given and command obeyed into the continuity between the command given and the entire sequence of commands, including the one obeyed by whichever human first seized the center. Sameness throughout the command can be ensured through detailed implementation, leaving no room for deviation, but also therefore leaving no margin for error in the face of contingencies. Or it can be ensured through a minimization of accompanying instructions, in which case the center signifies through the donation of the subject to the center: the donation of the very signifying capacities borrowed from the center.

Insofar as a social crisis is transcended or resolved, it is done so through a retrieval of the originary scene. The retrieval of the originary scene means an assembling by deferred desire for some central object—the central object that is the most dangerous in the given social setting. Scripture and metaphysics are such retrievals of the originary scene within the crisis of the ancient imperial orders. The organization of communities around intellectual practices resistant to sacrificial mobilization, around saints, around wise men, around dialogue focused on conceptual paradoxes, around sacred texts and revelatory events: these are the disciplinary orders of late antiquity which retrieve the practices of deferral and revise and neutralize decadent sacrificial practices. The study of these disciplinary orders is itself productive of disciplinary orders. While these disciplinary orders of the Axial Age[1] exposed the decrepitude of divine kingship, they operated exclusively through a withdrawal from questions of power. Only this way could they sustain their practices of deferral, but this limits their usefulness as models for solving the problem of restoring a kind of working amity between the signifying center and the occupied, governing center. The need to solve that problem is imposed upon all of us, because if there would be one thing we could come close to unanimous agreement on, it would probably be that there is no space of withdrawal from power struggles. We are all of us implicated in various forms of direct and indirect violent centralization, and all of our language is unmistakably marked by this violence. Just try and speak about any but the most trivial (and even, increasingly, what we might have considered trivial) matters in a "nonpartisan" way that doesn't divide the world up into friends and enemies, that doesn't isolate those against whom the power of the state should be deployed. Try not to speak in terms of inviolable rights perpetually under threat by one tyrant or another—and see what you are left able to say.

It's therefore not surprising that modern liberal thought is allergic to discussions of power: power is either held or used "legitimately," that is, according to some "super-sovereign" concept to which the actual ruler is beholden, or it is used "tyrannically." How it is actually used seems beside the point. In order to make the point, we can begin by pointing out that power comes from the center, and the center comes from deferral. Insofar as someone occupies the center of a scene, that person wields power.

---

1 This discussion is indebted to David Graeber's discussion in *Debt: The First 5,000 Years.*

We could use these concepts to carry out very micro-level power analyses: if one person, however otherwise irrelevant and ignored, becomes the center of attention in however small a group, however briefly, to that extent that person exercises power. The exercise of power involves, first, exhibiting deferral: when others give in to some mimetic contagion, like panic, whoever is able to resist that contagion and model another way of responding to the situation is exercising power. In so resisting, the agent turns himself into a center of attention—he has done something others couldn't or didn't think to, and so everyone will now look to see what he does next. It is also the case that in making himself the center of attention, whoever exercises power makes himself liable to convergent attention and violent centralization. He has made an implicit promise to provide an alternate response to panic, or surrender, and his next moves will reveal whether he can keep those promises. His fellows may judge wrongly: what they take to be a failure to redeem a promise might in fact be more acts of deferral, laying the groundwork for some plan that they are less capable of seeing than he is—that is, their panic can overtake them once again. This is why the second component of power is representing the desires and resentments that emerge within the group—that have in fact been generated by the exercise of power. One member of the group wants to drop out, another sabotages it out of spite, yet another engages in petty criticism of decisions that have not yet been given a chance to bear fruit, another gives off the sense, more or less unmistakably, that he would really have a better way of seeing us through this new difficulty. Exercising power involves not only blocking these moves but using them to continue renewing the group's relation to the center: whatever project has led to the articulation of the team.

Only one person can occupy the center at a time, just like only one person can speak at a time in a conversation. Part of occupying the center is delegating roles to one's confederates; by the same logic as single occupancy of the center, each other member of the team, at any one time, can only occupy one position in the hierarchy. So, if there is the one that goes first, there is then one that goes second, one that goes third, fourth, and so on. If the hierarchy branches off in different ways, this sequence is reproduced in each "branch." We can call this structure "centered ordinality":

each gesture toward the center, or each assertion of centrality, initiates the ordering mentioned above. Insofar as it doesn't, it turns out not to have been an assertion of centrality. Leadership can therefore be reduced to the maintenance of centered ordinality: leadership is successful to the extent that everyone knows their place in the order at a given point in the process, and that there is no gap between actual order and nominal order. This is what power is—having theorized that, I can address the fairly obvious fact that the exercises of power we see on a daily basis often don't correspond closely to this model. If an institution deviates too much from this model, it will cease to function—even highly corrupt institutions must have at least an inner circle, or enough mid-level groups, where shared goals and a clear chain of command are sustained. The question, though, is how to diagnose such deviations, which seem far more common than the "norm." We can reduce the question to, "what disrupts centered ordinality?" On the most immediate analytical level, we would look to some discrepancy between nominal and actual order.

But such discrepancies and imperfections are inevitable, and as long as they are marginal they can be addressed within the process itself. These disruptions become pervasive and chronic disruptions of centered ordinality because of some discrepancy between the occupied center and the signifying center. Let's imagine a team formed improvisationally in some emergency—say, escaping from a burning building. One individual seems to know the way out, so others follow and listen to him. On the fly, he delegates tasks—you look to see if anyone is left upstairs, you check to see if there's something we can use as a ladder, you find a way to help the injured, etc.; the scene has a clear center—to sustain the cooperation necessary to get as many people to safety as possible. Let's say they succeed—then what? Obviously the group can dissolve, as everyone goes back to their own lives. But let's say they have reasons to sustain themselves as a group—maybe this building was their home, and now they want to rebuild it, and to do so in a way that makes it less vulnerable to fire. The person who got them out of the building may not be the best person to take charge of this new, radically different, task. They may elect someone to oversee the rebuilding—in that case, the one in charge is formally subordinate to the group, or the majority. This can easily be the case without a formal election, because informal cooperation will still be necessary, and could be withheld in ways that would be difficult to account for. Now, to the extent that the one in charge confers upon the assembly the power to confer power upon him, we have a discrepancy: the task of the new leader is not to build the building, but to maintain a majority among those he is serving. Every decision he makes now has a double meaning: on the one hand, it needs to contribute to the rebuilding; on the other hand, it has to help him to keep majority support.

From the standpoint of the group, the need to have someone in charge still seems to be the default assumption; however, the more any particular leader seems dispensable at the whim of the group, the more this default assumption slides into scapegoating, and the generation of fantasies, themselves subject to debates and power struggles, of other arrangements. Perhaps a majority can be created for ruling by committee, or for taking turns, or even for a kind of anarchy in which each individual simply picks up the slack wherever it seems necessary to do so. Indeed, any of these alternatives might work as long as a certain threshold of resentment is not reached, but once that threshold is approached, the default assumption will be restored, only in a less explicit way, because it is now "controversial." Decisions will now increasingly be made by whoever is best able to mobilize a majority, according to whatever process of determining majorities the group uses; at a certain point decisions will be made more by those who are able to leverage the process of determining majorities. No doubt very skillful leaders can find ways to represent and redirect even the manifold resentments generated by this process, but it will become less likely that such leaders will emerge and survive. Now, some reasoning must be providing for a particular way of selecting and replacing leaders. Why a "majority"? A majority of whom? There may be many ways of slicing up the potential electorate. Some new agency must be constructed so as to make some sense out of the process (think of all the situations where it would be patently absurd to let the majority decide something)—say, the "people." The "people" must be anthropomorphized, provided with thought and agency. It has conflicts; it changes its mind; it gets fooled and manipulated—a wide range of narratives regarding this new fictional entity will be created. Deliberations regarding selecting a leader no longer concern the best way to rebuild, but determining what the "people" want—what they really want, not what some demagogue or slick operator manages to make them think they want. Of course, all along there was another option: let the guy who got everyone out of the building choose his successor. He can do it in consultation with whoever might be able to help him decide; he can establish a process for providing the group with veto power. He might not be the best person to decide; he might get it wrong—but, at least, there would be a clear decision, made by someone who has demonstrated some competence in one crucial area, along with a willingness to take risks for the group. We can at least assume he'll want to do the best he can, and he's likely to be willing to rely on the help of the community to supplement his own shortcomings. If he gets it wrong, it may be in choosing the second, third or fourth best, rather than the twentieth best—so, the building might go up in the end, with those who could have done a better job gracefully taking on their allotted roles and maybe over-producing a bit. So, secure power places a premium on continuity in leadership; if having the actual leader serve some metaphysically "realer" entity is the highest priority, power cannot be secured, and we have all the institutional pathologies we are familiar with. The problem here results from what might seem a small slippage: any leader does depend upon those he leads, who must therefore in some sense willingly participate; but this willing participation, or donation, can only be meaningfully performed when addressed to the competencies of each, not to some presumed ontologically prior identity of them all. In the first case each tries to align with the center, while in the latter all try, in what is an inevitably circular manner, to define the center. This still leaves us with the question, which we are still some way from answering (or from showing how an answer is solicited from the signifying center), of whether I should obey this man; but it shifts the focus of the question from "this man" to the specific command.

Now, the foundation of the community, which is the origin of leadership successions, is different than the assembling of a team—in the latter case, the existence of the community is already taken for granted. So, I could leave the question of sacrality, or the signifying center in its most compelling form, mostly aside.

This must be addressed so as to reconcile the signifying center and the occupied center. Gans identifies "significant" and "sacred" on the originary scene, and I follow him here—even with the decline of the sacred, there can never be any decline in "significance." Once the center has been humanly occupied, the problem becomes determining, or knowing, that the center as occupied is the same center as the center as signifying. The originary center "tells" the group to defer appropriation; as exchanges with the center multiply, as the imperatives from the center are extended beyond the ritual scene, the center becomes richer with activity: beings at the center appear and disappear, make demands, distribute rewards, and deliberate and fight amongst themselves regarding how to do so. Once a human occupies the center, he becomes part of these ritual exchanges and mythical narratives: he ascends to power, acts, and distributes in prescribed ways, with the collaboration of central beings. Systems of signs are generated that have to be "read" in order to order these prescribed activities in the right ways. A priestly class of specialists devotes itself to reading these signs, which is to say to conveying the meanings of the signifying center to the occupied one. The continuity of power is still presupposed—even if the priests are, on rare occasions, actually choosing the occupant of the center, they are certainly not determining the form of that occupancy. The reading of signs is as ritualized as the ruling, even if the need to interpret opens up some space to deal with "exceptional" circumstances. Anyone might be able to imagine that the man who happened to be king now might not prove to be the most "qualified" if a kingdom-wide "job search" were to be held, but he has ascended and now rules through a complex, time-tested process that draws upon the talent and accumulated means of the entire community in a way that would not be replicable if there were a constant search for someone who might be "better" in the abstract.

XI

TALK OF THE
CENTER

All of this becomes problematic once sacrifice has ended, and imperative exchange has given way to what we could call "interrogative imperativity": rather than giving to the center what it instructs you to, and requesting that it fulfill its promises in exchange (one of your goats for another year of the river flowing within its banks), each individual, as non-sacrificable center, takes himself to be asked who he is (what makes him the same "him") in giving himself over to the center completely. In other words, the relation between center and margins becomes incommensurable—nothing could equate to what each of us has been given by the center, so only absolute devotion to the center can suffice. In most everyday lives, imperative exchange is still the norm, insofar as we act on the assumption of commensurability between what we give and what we receive; but imperative exchange is ultimately incoherent (all of the exchanges don't really "add up," if looked at closely), and the incommensurable donation to the center answers to the perceived anomalies in the exchange system. There is no more hierarchy of beings at the center which orders an earthly hierarchy in which each will find his place. One's place in relation to the signifying center is fundamentally questionable, even if one's relation to the occupied center is not—hence the discrepancy. This questionableness is what all those new disciplines are interested in, and if they start off on the margins and uninterested in power, once they come to replace the old priestly classes this changes. The ruler must himself be ruled by God's law, and then by "Reason," and then as a "servant of the people," and so on—

all concepts controlled by the disciplines, upon whom the king is as dependent as he previously was upon the priestly classes. (The distinction between king and priest indicates a fundamental split between occupied center and signifying center, one that even precedes sacral kingship, going back to the distinction between shamans and tribal leaders.) Now, the government must be ruled by "political science," "international law," or "economics"—only concepts drawn from these and other disciplines can make rule legitimate. Even the majority, the nominal "sovereign," must yield to these super-sovereignties, which is to say those who interpret them, who "rule" the disciplines. The disciplines can't rule directly—the head of state in any country is still the successor, however distant, of some last king who ruled over that territory, and therefore all the kings and occasional queens preceding him. But that nominal occupant of power is at the center of struggles by power centers, leveraging the results of the disciplines' inquiries to influence as much as possible the decisions of the sovereign, which is to say, to deploy the sovereign against the enemies of the discipline in question. The discrepancy between signifying and occupied center will generate struggles over the occupancy of the center, which struggles then inform and divide the disciplines.

Just as any contemporary ruler is a distant inheritor of the earliest sacral kings, the contemporary disciplines have descended from metaphysics and scripture.[1] They continue the same project of eliminating the discrepancy between the signifying center and the occupied center. The target of metaphysics and scripture alike was "mythology," and this too has continued, from the Enlightenment critique of Christianity as "mythology" to Marxist critiques of "ideology" and more contemporary attempts to dismantle "whiteness." We can think about this as a continual process of replacement and reconfiguration. Mythology explains our ritual practices as commemorating or being commanded by beings of the center. The initial move in "demythification," then, is to replace the activities of beings of the center with those of beings of the margins. It was humans that created the myths and the rituals. How and why, though? If you are attacking some myth, or

---

1   See my "Introduction to Disciplinarity," *Anthropoetics* XX, No. 2, Spring 2015; and "Generative Anthropology as the One Big Discipline," *Anthropoetics* XXIV, No. 2, Spring 2019.

something you are going to call "myth," it is because it supports the power of someone you would like to see have less power: your enemy or opponent. Myth supports the tyrant; demythification aids the liberation of those inhabiting some pre-political space (embodied in some internal scene of representation) that is violated by the tyrant. But each victory over myth and tyranny installs a new tyrant supported by a new mythology—that pristine pre-political space can never be actualized. Thus, with its victory, the discourse of demythification becomes, in turn, the myth to be dethroned. The weapons don't have to change very much: much of what could be said, in attacking monarch and church in the name of the people and freedom, could be said in attacking the bourgeoisie, or the white, or the male, or the straight, claiming to represent that fictional entity "the people," in the name of the proletariat, the colonized, the woman, the gay, the transgender. The basis of the new liberating discourse is never provided, and can't be provided: it is enough that it is other than, othered by, and opposed to, that which it exposes as "mythical." Still, today, even the soberest, data-driven study in the most moderate political science department of, say changes in "public opinion," is nothing more than an attempt to demythify one belief about "the people" and replace it with a new myth, that of "public opinion." (Or one mythical form of public opinion by another.) For that matter, all public discourse in modern democracies can be reduced to each side purporting to demythify the other.

Myths are the products of sociality that can't be recognized as such and the problem of a post-sacrificial order is not to restore sacrality but, rather, to make discourse and practice directly, explicitly and completely social. Directly, explicitly and completely social means: a defender, representative and emissary of the center, "all the way down." Our constructions of the center reveal our constructedness by the center, which means that we are never outside of some tradition of centeredness. We are used to thinking about traditions in terms of rituals and institutions, but the deepest and most difficult to examine traditions lie in language itself. We can see how difficult from the work of the linguist Anna Wierzbicka, who has taken up the Sapir-Whorf hypothesis and, one must say, successfully resolved it. Wierzbicka has discovered a set of what she calls "Natural Semantic Primes"—that is, words, exact translations of which exist in every language. Another way of defining and testing the primes is to say they are words that can't be paraphrased by other words, without those other words ultimately having to be paraphrased using the primes themselves. Now, the existence of words that exist in every language might seem to be the exact opposite of what Whorf (in particular) claimed, which is that every language constructs reality for its users in a distinctive way that is not translatable into other languages. But what the primes enable Wierzbicka to do is to prove Whorf's claim regarding the relativity of language. By translating words from one language into the primes, it becomes possible to show precisely how those words are different in meaning from words that seem synonymous in other languages.[2]

Wierzbicka's studies have, understandably, focused on English, the present-day global lingua franca. She focuses on what would seem to be some of the most "universal" and "obvious" words in English—words that not only seem to have intuitively natural meanings but are taken to provide us with a direct access to reality—like "sense," "evidence," and "experience" (and many others), and shows that it is precisely these words that have no equivalents in other languages. Even more, she traces these words back to their origins—in the case of the above mentioned, and some other related ones, almost completely from the philosophical works of John Locke. In effect, when we're speaking English, and putting forth our theories of (and justifying foreign policy based on) the "rule of law," "empiricism," "universal rights" and "utilitarianism," and so on, we're effectively speaking the rather provincial dialect of Lockean. Seeing language anew through Wierzbicka, just like seeing the metalanguage of literacy through Olson, has a startling, demystifying effect that seems similar to other "demythifications." They are different, though, because they point us back to language, and therefore to the constitutive center, rather than some presumably self-sustaining "human" margin. For the discourses of demythification, the world needs to be set "right-

2 Wierzbicka has, over more than 40 years, published a very great number of books and essays, but I would recommend starting with her work on English, which she herself seems to see as especially important, given English's status as the de facto lingua franca: *Imprisoned in English: The Hazards of English as a Default Language*; *English: Meaning and Culture*; and *Experience, Evidence and Sense: The Hidden Cultural Legacy of English.*

side up" by showing how the divine depends on the human, the ruler on the ruled, the intellectual on the material. For anthropomorphics, the problem is very different: here, the problem is to constitute our utterances on a scene, with a center. We understand that all we're ever doing is iterating the originary scene, in increasingly complex ways because we must incorporate anomalies and contingencies (mistakes) generated by previous scenes, and we must keep retrieving and ensuring our continuity recursively with previous scenes. It's also helpful to keep in mind that that is all anyone is ever doing—all we can do is place ourselves on more differentiated scenes in the constitution of which we can display ever more of our contribution. The implications of Wierzbicka's primes help to clarify what this means. The effect of a Wierzbickean analysis is, at first glance, odd. Once you have taken a word, like "experience," or "embarrassment," and shown that its meaning entails a particular relation between people thinking, people seeing, people knowing, people knowing that others see them, people not wanting others to see them like that, people thinking about what they feel, people wanting others to know that they feel this way, and so on, you are done. Unlike most discourses in the social sciences (but like Ludwig Wittgenstein's analyses of linguistic forms as "forms of life" in his *Philosophical Investigations*) we don't have a universalizable inner structure upon which a lot of irrelevant details hang. We have the word itself, as an articulation of practices, within a specific tradition, with its history of uses. You're not provided with a way of stepping outside of the word (any other words you would step outside of it into would be subject to the same treatment), but are given an opportunity to see its complexity as a distinctive, centered way of seeing thinking, knowing, feeling, wanting, and so on within a given community.

Wierzbicka's primes dismantle any assumption of the transparency of any language, including those of the human sciences, more radically than what are by now standard invocations of the (race, class, gender, sexuality...) positionality of the inquirer. If you think you can deconstruct a discourse in the human sciences because the maleness of the author, or the field, or that subset of the field, shapes the discourse in exclusionary ways, and even if you add to this the whiteness, straightness, First Worldness, etc., of the disciplinary position, you are still assuming the possibility of some unmarked, properly intersectional liberatory position at the end of the chain. With Wierzbicka's analytics, there's no end of the chain. Wierzbicka herself is primarily interested in preventing ethnocentrism, and, perhaps, the globally dominant Anglo ethnocentrism in particular from interfering with the possibility of communication and shared inquiry across linguistic lines. But translations into the primes can only be an after the fact practice: we couldn't directly communicate in the primes. And this leaves unaddressed what also follows from Wierzbicka's confirmation of the Sapir-Whorf hypothesis: that the distinctiveness of each language is a source of discovery in its own right, and not just "noise" interfering with what might otherwise be clear communication. If we could all manage to speak in the primes as our native language, the world of thinking would be terribly impoverished as a result.

I don't mean to suggest Wierzbicka would deny any of this, but she doesn't emphasize it anywhere that I am aware of, and I am emphasizing it because my interests run elsewhere than Wierzbicka's. If we are able to see languages as something like disciplinary spaces themselves, which organize reality in such a way as to bring certain things to attention, and to in effect construct those "elements" of reality by occluding other elements, we can treat the disciplinary spaces of the human sciences as idioms within a larger language, rather than as transparent metalanguages that bring us ever closer to a secular, demythified, liberated reality. The disciplines, we could say, are those spaces set up to inquire specifically into what words, sentences and discourses mean across the field of language—including within the disciplines themselves. The question, then, is how do we speak about what words mean without some kind of metalanguage that provides the implicitly mystified terms with a demystified meaning? There would be no inquiry into meaning if meaning wasn't called into question in some way—if there weren't, that is, some question of how to distinguish between normal and anomalous usage. The purpose of inquiry would then be less to adjudicate the terms of usage than to identify where the boundaries between what counts as normal or anomalous usage lie in specific practices, or fields of practice. Wierzbicka's natural semantic metalanguage would be very well suited for probing these boundary spaces. This is a metalanguage that is really more of what Bruno Latour has called an "infra language,"[3] which results from one discourse entering another.

I argued above that the human sciences have their origins in the establishment of the primacy of the declarative sentence effected by literacy and manifested, in the West, in metaphysics and scripture (synthesized in Christianity). The metaphysical discovery is that ostensive and imperative signs can be represented in declarative terms, and that representing them in declarative terms enables the declarative to control the ostensive and imperative: or, to put it in grammatical terms, to issue imperatives and generate ostensives. If we're talking, I can point to something—if, at some later point, that pointing needs to be represented for, say, legal purposes, my pointing to something gets redescribed in terms that would note my position, what I was likely able to see, what else was in the vicinity, and potentially much more (the state of my optic nerve, etc.) that would abstract my pointing from the ostensive situation. What I "really saw" is now better left in the hands of professionals who have categorized all the elements of "seeing something." The same is the case for imperatives: redescribing person A commanding person B to carry out some act raises the question (to be answered in further declaratives) of who person A and B are such that A can command B, and therefore whether that command was a "real" command (whether B obeyed it or not), which is to say issued by one person who is in a position to command that other person. And what does it mean to be in a position to command another?—one has been "authorized" to do so, and authorization implies terms of authorization, themselves inscribed in declarative sentences. To some extent, at least, issuing commands places you in conflict with those who will redescribe those commands in declarative terms: at the very least, those later descriptions will subject the command to criteria and calculations that could not possibly have been present to the one issuing the command in the original situation. The reason metaphysics needs to be dismantled is that the interests of metaphysics lie in ensuring that all imperatives and ostensives are controlled and guaranteed in advance by declaratives, and this is an infiltration and sub-

3 *Reassembling the Social: An Introduction to Actor-Network Theory*, 30.

version of the ostensive-imperative world. The declarative order in effect usurps the ostensive-imperative world by generating unacknowledged commands to those responsible for commanding. To say something like "that order would violate the protocols of this institution, which have in turn been established in accordance with domestic law passed pursuant to a particular international treaty, etc." is to say: you cannot issue this command; and it is to say this without being able to provide an alternative command that would meet the needs of that situation. One could say that those giving the commands can be trained in accord with procedures that internalize that declarative order, but this just means having the declarative order encroach more pervasively upon the ostensive-imperative world, without there being any reason to assume that the commands subsequently issued within that institution will be more appropriate for its purposes. And in the end, without preserving the integrity of the ostensive-imperative world, the declarative order is bereft of the meaning its inhabitants fantasize they can generate out of that order.

If the declarative sentence, for metaphysics, is the well-formed proposition that can be linked according to logical (definitional and grammatical) rules to other propositions and according to some "rules of evidence" to ostensive claims about reality (material or ideal), the declarative sentence, for scripture, is a narrative of the emergence of the individual as a center: a non-sacrificable center among other non-sacrificable centers, and therefore a center of responsibility. There is no need for the scriptural declarative to invade the ostensive-imperative world, as does the metaphysical declarative. To be told the story of a victim of centralizing violence is to be issued the imperative "don't commit such violence," and provided with a kind of map for how to avoid doing so; similarly, to be told the story of a saint who refrained from responding in kind to some violation and absented himself from potentially contagious desires and resentments is to be issued a command to imitate that kind of response to temptations to resentment. The problem for the scriptural declarative is that, due to its anti-imperial/meta-imperial origins, the only means it provides for distinguishing between proper and improper imperatives issued by power centers is in terms of whether those power centers defend the originating narrative of the authorizing scripture. If the power center is responsible for distinguishing between discourses issuing from, on the one hand, and deviating from, on the other hand, the authorizing narrative, rules must be constructed for establishing that distinction. The only way of establishing a body of rules is propositionally, which means that the scriptural world must rely upon the metaphysical declarative world. Once this happens, the imperatives issued by the metaphysical order will consistently override those issued within the scriptural order because the former has been set in judgment of the latter.

XII

THE CENTER
AND IMPERATIVE AUTHORITY

The civilizational problem we have here, at least in the Western world (and therefore the rest of the world, which has all been at least in part modeled on Western norms) is that of the imperatives issued from the highest power center, or the central authority. There is, in any community, a central authority, the final source of imperatives; and yet those imperatives are only worthy of being followed if the central authority is in accord with the signifying center: to put it more precisely, if the imperatives issued by the central authority are the same as those issued by the signifying center. As yet, no satisfactory way of ensuring this has been proposed, let alone implemented. This problem, I have suggested, dates back to the fall of sacral kingship (although I imagine I have made it clear that retaining sacral kingship, much less restoring it, cannot be considered an option), which makes it a very longstanding one. How to "legitimate" the central authority, or the sovereign (without, for now, getting into the tangled history of that concept), without creating an "imperium in imperio," or a "realer" sovereign than the actual sovereign? This, what I have been calling, "super-sovereign," must itself be represented—by a Church, or a parliament, a constitution, or a judiciary, or an international body—and representation either recreates the same problem over again (what legitimates the Church or the judiciary, who interprets the constitution?) which in turn opens a kind of loophole through which power struggles can be waged. If the Church or the judiciary is to be the ultimate arbiter, then if one wants to counter the king or president one seeks control of the

Church or judiciary, or Church doctrine or legal theory, which, in turn, requires control over the universities, seminaries and law schools. Liberalism is the political theory justifying this state of affairs, which means that the purpose of liberalism is to ensure that no one ever knows who decides anything. Can there be any reason to believe that decisions will be made and implemented better this way?

The civilizational project I am proposing for the disciplines, then, is the one I suggest they have really been pursuing all along: inquiring into the meaning of imperatives issued by central authority (which are of course transmuted into other imperatives along various chains of command, and studied with regard to needed means of implementation, including the distribution of resources, the training and employment of personnel, and so on). I can make this more precise: the proper inquiry of the human sciences is the difference between the imperatives issued by central authority and the imperatives obeyed by lower authorities. Imperatives are performatives: they transform, rather than describe, reality. No imperative, however carefully and informatively formulated, however close in time and space to its implementation, can ever completely account for the conditions of implementation. So, if we assume the existence of some central authority in any community, the most minimal assumption we can make regarding what constitutes a central authority, is that imperatives coming from that authority both precede and supersede all other imperatives. Which is to say those imperatives are always to be obeyed—to do otherwise is to align oneself with another, potential, more or less imminent, central authority, even (especially, really) if one disobeys in the name of one or another super-sovereign concept ("human rights," or whatever). To disobey is irresponsible and therefore immoral, because it denies and obscures the direct sociality of discourse by invoking some internal scene of representation, upon which the "merits" of differing sources of legitimacy can be assessed. Homing in on the difference between imperative issued and imperative obeyed brings questions of morality and responsibility into focus far more effectively. It is in one's filling the imperative "gap" that one provides moral and intellectual feedback to superiors and ultimately to the central authority. A bad, or, say, "infelicitous," imperative, is simply one that can't be effectively fulfilled, either on its own terms or because it conflicts with some equally authoritative imperative coming from the center. Even a very good government is likely to pose such dilemmas to its people—perhaps even more so, insofar as a good government would confer more responsibilities on its people, supervise less closely, and therefore issue less specified commands. Of course, a bad government would pose these dilemmas in much direr ways. If we assume that these dilemmas, which would always be posed in unique ways, must be resolved as best as possible without ever imagining one could disobey the central authority, the field of political, moral and social inquiry becomes very rich indeed.

So, an inquiry into meaning is an inquiry into the difference between imperative issued and imperative obeyed, including how that difference is registered in the declarative order, itself taken as the study of the ostensive-imperative world: more precisely, the study of which hierarchy of imperatives will produce the greatest ostensive yield (the practices, places and things that best reveal our social being). The difference in question is a product of the element of "inappropriateness" constitutive of any imperative: again, even within the most tightly structured chain of command in the most closed environment, there will be something in any imperative that can't be fulfilled as commanded (as imagined by the commander). As the recipient of a command, you become a center, along with bearing and presenting the centrality of whoever has issued the command. The mistakenness of the imperatee is a breach in the order of signs (linguistic presence) which initiates the convergence of attention upon that imperatee, and depending upon the source and scope of that covering attention, upon the imperator as well. As attention converges upon you, there are two possible responses: one, you can try to deflect the attention elsewhere, which involves evacuating yourself as the one receiving an imperative; two, you can convert that convergent attention into shared attention to the range of problems raised by the best implementation of the imperative (our "selves" are essentially articulations, in some proportion, of these two types of response). This conversion involves ostensive, imperative and declarative dimensions: it involves "holding" oneself a certain way—for example, not reacting symmetrically or in kind to accusations; it involves showing oneself to be following orders and issuing various imperatives (from modest requests to imperious commands) oneself; and it involves, invoking and enacting the origin of the declarative form itself, predicating some object (an individual, a situation) that could provoke violent convergence, and doing so in such a way as to make the object signify a way of refraining from such convergence. Through these pedagogical and moral practices the signifying center is brought to bear on the occupied center, and the imperative gap closed.

The inquiry initiated by potential or imminent convergence toward imperative mistakenness involves an unfolding of the practice in question into its constitutive practices. This practice of inquiry has something in common, then, with any social analytics, which will, for example, in explaining a ritual, identify the "components" of that ritual (the actors, the means, the rules, the connection to other practices, etc.), with it then being possible to "break down" or abstract those components into components of their own, until we reach the terms of an anthropological ontology. What is different in anthropomorphics is that the inquiry is explicitly set on the scene of inquiry itself. The origin and essence of the declarative sentence is that it provides the capacity to represent events happening at different times and places (and different times and places than that where and when the sentence itself is uttered) in a single present. The original declarative traces the transformation of a demand into a request for information regarding the demanded object, that is, a question, which is answered with a negation (not here). An originary ontology of the declarative preserves the negative ostensive by composing the declarative world out of declaratives that both construct a chain from the ostensive-imperative articulations conditioning the possibility of this declarative order and by indicating, issuing, tacit imperatives that operate within that world. This makes the present tense predominant in anthropomorphic inquiry. What has happened in the past is available in the present because memories, records and ramifications of that past are ostensively available in the present: the possibility of a propositional order, which we owe to metaphysics, is redeemed in the possibility of always adding a new increment of ostensive inheritance that would establish a new past from which hitherto unseen or overseen or underseen memories, records and ramifications can be made present. In thusly representing the confluence of events, each one of which can be more fully represented in its mimetic structure and articulation of convergent and shared attention, the declarative order being constructed contributes to closing the imperative gap by modifying that inheritance and thereby issuing a tacit imperative to obey the order one way as opposed to another.

XIII

DECLARATIVE ORDER
AND THE CENTER

Remember that the metalanguage of literacy I have extracted from David Olson's work aims at constructing a simulated scene upon which the writer and readers stand, observing whatever is represented by the writer. The scene of classical prose is, then, readerly rather than writerly—it avoids drawing attention to the scene of writing itself, which is really a sketch of a succession of scenes upon which given signs are iterated in different ways. Classic prose solves a problem that the invention of writing creates, but which is really just the expansion of a field upon which a problem constitutive of language itself is displayed and played out. On the originary scene, the most urgent problem as the scene takes shape, is for all, or "enough," participants to be able to ascertain, or know, simply, that they are all in fact issuing the newly discovered and invented sign. This is a process in which the participants transition from attention (giving and receiving it in uncertain oscillation) to intention (finding means for identifying and controlling the attention of others). As the primary problem on the originary scene, this is therefore also the primary problem of the human. To put it bluntly, we are always doing nothing other than trying to determine whether "we" are in fact issuing the same sign. This is a real problem which can never be solved once and for all because, of course, it never is the same sign—to some degree, every repetition of a sign modifies its meaning, or its range of possible uses, in some way. So, the problem is establishing sameness in the midst of difference. A disciplinary space is where we make this attempt.

Metalanguage is a way of solving this problem, and it's not surprising that the masters of writing would have found this solution to be an appropriate one to the problem of potentially infinite dissemination. Metalanguage establishes rules for the proper use of signs. The metalanguage of literacy, as I pointed out earlier, defines words, which is to say, abstracts from the mass of language use those specific ways in which one is allowed to use particular words; it establishes rules of grammar and logic, which essentially function to keep the declarative order at a sufficient distance from the ostensive-imperative world so as to avoid contamination; and it establishes broader disciplinary rules, and rules of genre and style aimed at guaranteeing the transparency of discourse for those inhabiting the metalanguage of literacy, or those fluent in the prevailing literate idioms. If we've established rules for using words, for grammar, for genre and style, and, indeed, for checking and updating these rules and adjudicating specific cases, we can examine the differences of specific texts in a contained way. What, though, if each time we read a text, the proper use of words, grammatical rules, logic, generic and stylistic norms, were all up for grabs at each point along the way of the reading practice, and in shared inquiries into texts? In that case, the sameness of identity of a particular sign could only be affirmed on a particular scene of inquiry, in which one participant is able to say something like "if we take these words to be usable in this way, and accept the possibility that this other mode of grammar and logic might 'work,' and entertain the possibility that genre and stylistic norms are being used here in order to produce effects beyond the consideration of those responsible for maintaining those norms, then the text here would be doing X"; and another participant would be able to follow up on that with another possible articulation of definitional, grammatical, logical, generic and stylistic practices in this text, but also, now, in the "critical" practice of inquiry that can use this practice of textuality as a model. The starting point of such an inquiry would still be the metalanguage of literacy and the narrower metalanguages of specific disciplinary practices, but now, in applying those terms, either inappropriately, or to an object one shows (or helps) to resist appropriate application, the application of those terms, along with the modifications effected through passing them through the prism of the constructed object, is now to the space of inquiry itself. What we have in that case is a kind of transdisciplinary infralanguage, in which the identity of the sign must be "authenticated" on each scene of inquiry (even the signs marking a scene of inquiry must be authenticated on a scene of inquiry, both within and outside of the scene of inquiry to be marked). This takes us to the end of metaphysics by retrieving the origin and vocation of the declarative sentence prior to its hypostatization by the metalanguage of literacy, of which metaphysics is merely an occluded version. That vocation is to determine the precise distance at which we need to hold the ostensive-imperative world so as to prioritize the many imperatives coming our way so that we represent to each other the way their originating center would like us to obey them.

Scriptural declarative orders involve narratives that take us from the violent convergence of attention, or violent centralization, to the conversion of that convergence into shared attention directed at the mimetic crisis, or the unresolved mistakenness of the ostensive-imperative world, that led to the convergence in the first place. Scriptural narratives effect this conversion through the hearing and heeding of an absolute imperative, the foundation of what Philip Rieff calls the "interdictory authority," which creates "renunciatory disciplines of obedience to god-terms beyond the figure of the charismatic figure."[1] Here, the absolute imperative is the imperative to devote yourself to the signifying center by interposing yourself between the convergent attention and the potential sacrifice. Let's take this one step further and say that the absolute imperative is to name the potential sacrifice, which is to say surround it ostensively so as to render it immune to sacrificial intentions. Naming something in the world as a moral act is the most originary of signifying gestures. Historically, scriptural narratives have displaced sacrificial and mythical ones by constructing an "emperor" that necessarily transcends all world emperors, actual or possible, because He has created the world and everything in it. A point by point "refutation," or really, satirical subversion, beyond anything we would probably be able to reconstruct at this point, of all previous ritual, mythological and imperial orders was required to accomplish this. We looked before at the impasse at which scripture eventually arrives: its implicit

---

1 *Charisma: The Gift of Grace, and How it has been Taken from Us*, 229.

anti-imperialism dispossesses it of any means of resisting incorporation as a "super-sovereignty" that provides the resources for endless denunciations of "tyranny" in the name of some inviolable internal center. We could say this process is, in fact "history"—history, that is, is the record of the replacement of one empire after another in anticipation of the establishment of the final, true empire, that would be direct subordination to God, but then, also, to some version of the authentically unpolluted human. History, then, has exhausted itself in the antinomic agencies of contemporary liberalism, where the genuinely stripped bare human that can be the only source of legitimacy is nothing but sheer opposition to whatever norms make social functioning possible.

But the imperative to redeem scripture can be obeyed at least as well as that to redeem the propositional order created by metaphysics. What we retrieve from scripture is what we can call "listening to the center," which is to say developing disciplinary spaces for discerning the most pertinent forms taken by the absolute imperative. Like scripture, this requires narrative far more than propositional forms. Let's start with the appearance of mistakenness in what we can call the "in-ordering" of an imperative (the effort to create the order extending from the imperative, to act within the order). Any crisis begins with a command, a demand, a request, an injunction, a prohibition, an insistence, etc., that is going unfulfilled. The "size" of the crisis will depend on the agencies involved, their relative power, the urgency and scope of the imperative, and so on—even if not necessarily in any obvious way. But at any size, the crisis begins by being placed in some declarative, narrative form: person or people X did something/are doing something. An event is represented, and an event "behind" that event: what's happening is shadowed by what is "really" happening. The narrative rewires the ostensive and imperative circuitry: you're looking here, but the signs you are looking at really point there; you are finding it incumbent to act in one way, but the situation requires that you act another way. The surface is bubbling with ostensives and imperatives—simply knowing what to look at and from what angle, and what the situation "demands," itself "demands" one seek out a higher imperative that would supersede all of these. But this means that one is already following the imperative to seek out a higher imperative; which, further, depends on the ostensive assumption that that higher impera-tive is there to be found. And that ostensive assumption must be right—even finding oneself disappointed at the end, and re-nouncing the search for higher imperatives, would have one fol-lowing the imperative to not seek out higher imperatives (and, a narrower imperative designating the precise imperative level at which one stops seeking higher).

So, when a narrative represents imperative mistakenness, we know a higher imperative will reorder the disordered imperative space. In the representations of the scene of imperative mistaken-ness, the participant can hear imperatives generated on that scene itself—imperatives that sustain and accelerate the scene of con-vergent, violent centralization by pointing out more confirmatory details and compelling each participant to take action that further locks him into the scene. "If you refuse to see what that means, that means you don't belong here"—that is, you belong with the victim. These imperatives can be recognized by their paradoxical form, that of the vicious circle. In the aftermath of such a scene, effort will have to be put into controlling all subsequent represen-tations of it: everyone on the scene will have to have been acting directly pursuant and proportionately to some immediate provo-cation to which response could not be delayed. And one can see signs of this on the scene already. In any representation of such a scene, even the most inciteful one, any participant can also see signs that suggest that deceleration is possible. The very existence of such signs rebuts the incitement. "See if there are further like signs" is the absolute imperative here. If you listen to it, the imper-ative becomes both more precise, telling you where to look, and more expansive, telling you to show others these signs, or, really, showing others they have already seen them. Even on a scene where immediate action is in fact urgently necessary, there must be some margin of uncertainty with regard to which action is best, even in split-second decisions. So, even in a genuine emergency, the capacity to decelerate enhances response-ability. A narrative starting from the element of deceleration within an acceletory frame will uncover more signs suggesting deceleration, and sub-tler distinctions, for example, between signs that presented as de-celetory but really served the purpose of incitement. Subsequent narratives would become further differentiated, to the point of refusing to converge attention even upon those most unambiguously accelerating on the scene, preferring to explore what they might have taken to be deceleratory imperatives to be followed. If punitive action needs to be taken, and accounted for after the fact, it is taken, however severe, in such a way as to reveal, foreground and enhance deceletory or inhibitory means of institutional and individual detection. This is how one listens to the center: the absolute imperative always tells one to hear more of imperatives to which one is exposed and to make them more consistent with each other: to name practices that bring into view things that issue those imperatives.

XIV

SKEWING TOWARD
THE CENTER

We inherit from metaphysics the possibility of replacing any word, phrase, gesture, or movement with a declarative sentence, or a string of declarative sentences, and then replacing the words in those sentences with strings of declarative sentences, and then doing the same with the very process of carrying out all of these replacements, and so on. Having declarative reframing at our disposal serves the purposes of deferral, which can in this way be organized in disciplinary spaces, which enable us to reframe accounts of events in new registers. The most minimal act of attention can thereby be spread out into a structure and history of practices limited only by the question prompting the inquiry, and the continual modulation of that question. We start with an event or utterance (but we only know events through utterances, and utterances are always an event), and at a certain point we will say we have determined what something means. Wierzbicka's analysis of words into the primes is an exemplary model for such post-metaphysical work within the declarative order, and I would hereby deem her thinking to be part of anthropomorphics. Still there is an interesting aporia in Wierzbicka's primes: there is, it seems, no prime word for "God," or "divine," or "sacred" or any related terms. This is certainly not due to any hostility or hesitation regarding the sacred on the part of Wierzbicka, who has written at least two books that translate Christian scripture into the primes. My assumption is that words for God and gods are too singularized, and it would be impossible, using Wierzbicka's exacting standards of identification, to claim that there are words in all languages referring to gods or the sacred that are the "same." Gods are always named, and names can't be in the primes. Wierzbicka, at any rate, never claims that the prime words are the earliest words, even if they are all certainly pre-literate. We can take them, I would suggest, as belonging to declarative language, leaving at least portions of the ostensive-imperative world untouched.

Wierzbicka's claim, which, again, I have no reason to contest, is that one way of identifying and verifying the primes is that they are words that cannot be paraphrased by other words without those other words having to be paraphrased, and so on, until we ultimately find our way back to the prime word. So, any attempt to paraphrase "think" would, if sufficiently thorough and rigorous, have to include the word itself in that paraphrase; this is not the case for a non-prime word like, say, "understand." The primes, then, are words that are understood or, to stick with the primes, known, intuitively; or, to put it in a way with less philosophical baggage, knowing how to use (or when to say) these words is simply part of being able to speak a language. In originary disciplinary spaces, though, things don't end there, because being able to gesture ostensively and issue and obey imperatives are also part of what it means to be able to speak a language. So, we can have non-tautological ways of saying what it means to "think," "know," "say," "want" and so on: they represent interactions at the center, which we iterate on the margin. The primes themselves are practices and this can be shown in a way that would be in principle available to Wierzbicka, even if to my knowledge she has never adopted it, and that is understanding the words in relation to each other. This will enable us to defend Wierzbicka's position while recognizing, for example, that the word "think," when someone says "I think," might mean something different than "think" in the question, "what do you think?"

Does "think" mean the same thing when someone, in response to a question of whether he'd like to go somewhere, says, "yes, I think so," as when someone says "if you think about it, you will agree with me"? The person who says "yes, I think so" is expressing a desire while simultaneously indicating some hesitation (there are other possibilities, of course), while the person saying "if you think about it…" is encouraging the other to engage in a cogitative process, to carry out a mental activity (but also, perhaps, reminding the other of consequences of "disagreeing"). We can make the meanings of "think" seem as different from each other in the respective cases as we like, but what I think vindicates Wierzbicka's model is that in both cases one *thinks* when one doesn't *know*, and one *thinks* before one *says*. And we can make the relations between the words even more precise if we consider when we would use one in an imperative rather than the other, or the limitations imposed upon using these words as imperatives. When do you command someone to think? When a decision has to be made, or a conclusion reached, and the person who has to make or reach it seems unprepared to do so. Which is a way of saying "think before you say you know," or "think before you do." Someone is commanded to "say something" when there has been ample time, or there is now no time, to "think." Of course, we have E.M. Forster's question, much beloved of writing instructors, "how do I know what I think until I see what I say," which suggests the simultaneity of thinking and saying. Even here, though, it seems that the saying does not so much coincide with as reveal the thinking which still, presumably, in some sense antedated it. At the very least, the saying can't precede any thinking, even if we speak about people speaking and acting before they have thought. When we accuse someone thus, we're limiting what we're willing to consider "genuine" thinking in this case, that is, using "thinking" in a restrictive way, while still preserving its priority over saying and doing (no one tells another he speaks or acts before he thinks as a compliment, even if one might advise another not to think "too much" before speaking or acting—which, again, presupposes the priority of thinking of these acts).

However such intra-prime analyses work out (is it meaningful to command or demand that someone *want* or *know* something? If not, what do we mean when we do so, as we all probably do on occasion?), I put these models of analysis forward as a contribution to the ongoing (it seems to be taking longer than it should) dismantling of the metaphysical reification of the declarative sentence, not in order to devalue (absurdly) the declarative sentence but to liberate its real "vocation." Wierzbicka's primes help free us from the metalanguage of literacy, but they also need to be freed from it. It can still be very difficult to resist the tendency, when hearing the words "think" or "know," to immediately convert that into a question like "what is real thinking/knowing," which in turn, as Wittgenstein knew, leads us to construct a "picture" of "thinking" and "knowing." Once we are drawing pictures of these activities, we invite arguments over their "thoroughness," or the "correctness" of this or that "detail." We try to "prove" that this or that "faculty" is an essential part of the "thought process," or that we haven't really "known" something until all the items on a checklist of what counts as "knowing" have been checked off. Do I need to convince you of how deeply rooted these habits of thought remain? The appropriation of Wierzbicka's primes by originary thinking allows us to maintain all the precision regarding determining the meaning of words that the most demanding analytical philosopher would insist upon, and as penetrating an analysis of the practices comprising any intellectual activity as any cognitive psychologist would hope for, without the kinds of pointless paradoxes that have been with us since Socrates wondered whether acts are good because the gods command them, or the gods command them because they are good. "Limiting" ourselves to the modest questioning of how the most minimally meaningful words are used in relation to each other will help generate a post-metaphysical human science.

We can remain with the declarative order for as long as we like, and there are substantial rewards for doing so: the purest form of the declarative order is mathematics, and when we are thinking genuinely scientifically, we are within the declarative. However delayed, though, the declarative must come home to the ostensive—even the most complex physics experiment carried out with the most intricate machinery must give the scientist something to see and point to—even if it's just a reading on a meter that is very distantly related to anything we might actually be able to engage with our senses. Moreover, science begins with a question, and a question is an extended imperative, and the imperative is extended because it turned out to be "inappropriate"—to not, in fact, have had the needed ostensive backing. The grounding of the declarative order in the ostensive-imperative world can also only be discussed (as anything can only be "discussed") in the declarative order, but nothing in the declarative order would ever impel its participants to initiate such discussions—which is why the metalanguage of literacy has ruled for so long. As Heidegger and Wittgenstein realized, it is mistakenness that opens up the declarative order to an inquiry into its ostensive and imperative roots. All of the paradoxes, aporias and anomalies with which the declarative order is rife, and which the metalanguage of literacy strives to hide from view, lead us back to the ostensive, and the only real paradox: that we name as already possessing the characteristics implicit in that name something that is only that thing because we have named it. *We*, not *I*; on a *scene*, not in a *mind*. (Whatever we imagine to be "internal" is really remembering of "external" scenes and rehearsal for future ones.) A discovery, scientific or otherwise, has been made once participants on a disciplinary scene see something that is simultaneously real and a product of the scene of inquiry (and all the modified practices and traditions of inquiry of which the scene is composed) that made it available to us.

XV

THE CENTER WITHOUT METALANGUAGE

The scene on which one sees what one is simultaneously shown has been the concern of scripture: this is what is entailed in a "revelation." On some level, we know that we ourselves don't completely produce what we see—in some sense we are "shown" it. This raises the question of how to name the one who shows it. On the one hand, unless we are literal believers, we know there is no one really showing it, and as social thinkers we can find some way of naming an agency that does so—"society," "tradition," "ideology," and so on. This all begs the question of how any of these entities could show us anything—wouldn't "believing" in them be just as questionable as believing in God? It is to fill this aporetic space that the human sciences rush in with all the faculties and capacities they deposit in the subject. I would have anthropomorphics fill the space with imperatives from the center and declaratives working out the performative gap of those imperatives so as to issue more precise imperatives, albeit always with a margin of mistakenness. I propose this as a theoretical language that should be more powerful than those indebted to the metalanguage of literacy. For one thing, it renders the self or subject directly and completely social and historical, rather than leaving us to figure out some way to "add" those "forces" afterward. Working imperatives through a declarative space so as to issue a more precisely targeted imperative produces an ostensive result the actor and observer can both see. That ostensive result is named, and any practice that is named is named as commanding a deferral of desire or resentment. Naming resists the erasure of the practice. Not everything that is named is "good," but the naming always proposes a good way of seeing that thing, as source of deferral rather than incitement. This is the case even with instances of naming that we must see, from the outside, as direct incitement—even those names defer some other even more imminent violence within that group, and could only meaningfully be countered with a better name. The result of the mobilizing of the declarative order so as to examine some practice that has become a "problem" is to return to that practice (or, perhaps, one of its "descendants," mutations, or incorporations) with a name.

All "speaking about" is naming, and all naming is the Name-of-God and enacted in the Name of God. So, every utterance is naming God in the name of God, and then we sort things out from there: how did God, or, let's say, the center, authorize and command that affixation of its name to that form of itself? Instead of asking why someone chose or decided to do or say something, which situates the prompting of the action somewhere within the subject (which is why we then have to add the social and historical parts afterward), an anthropomorphic disciplinary space has someone named or deemed by the center to deploy the name of the center. There's no claim to infallible knowledge of the intent of the center here—rather, this anthropomorphic idiom would be a way of initiating and sustaining collaborative inquiries into how we have come by the words we're using as part of using them. That doesn't mean we must all be linguists or philologists; it would just mean that our mode of interaction would presuppose that our words come to us, rather than from us. We are all of us centers, attracting convergent attention and open to shared attention; we are all of us directing attention to others and everything in the world as centers. So, on a kind of sliding scale, where is the "needle" between the drawing and directing of shared rather than convergent attention in any case? A study of names, which is a naming of names (we don't have to keep saying we are always naming but we can always remember that we are always naming), is a continual attempt to pinpoint where that needle is. The further the needle is toward the pole of shared attention, the more the name creates a space in which more naming is possible—when convergent attention, violent centralization, has not been sufficiently deferred, a narrow circle of names, applied in a way closely guarded (but therefore also, eventually, haphazard, productive of anomalies) is insisted upon. What is the advantage, other than familiarity, of speaking in terms of decisions, choices and capacities, subsequently to be supplemented by "society" and "history," over an idiom that has us speaking of transitions from attention to intention? In the latter case we can see the ways that just noticing some foreground against a background (to speak Gestalt) becomes a way of effecting some new relation between back and foreground—without needing to make a stop at a decision, or the will, or some cognitive capacity or moral deliberation (all of which things would be attention-intention "glides," in which a centered ordinality is joined).

Maybe it seems like I'm insisting on a metalanguage here, and a rather artificial and awkward one at that. What would be the point of "banning" perfectly serviceable words like "decide" and "choose," just because we might have some theoretical questions about the "substantives" which these verbs predicate? I'm just doing the kind of displacement work necessary when one disciplinary space enters into another—much that was taken for granted has to be explicitly revealed as anomalous. An anthropomorphic inquiry wants to settle down with all the commonly used words, most definitely including those like "decision" and "choice." But we don't have to keep using them exactly the same way—I haven't signed the linguistic or cultural equivalent of a non-disclosure form. When someone does something, and claims to have made a decision, there's no reason to deny it; what we can do, though, is try to figure out wherein, exactly, the decision lies. What is other than "decision" in an action, and where is the boundary between decision and non-decision? (Note that I am myself using terms like "try to figure out" here.) We can conduct thought experiments. Let's try and reduce the decision "point" to an absolute minimum by introducing as many determinants and making them as determinant as we can—bring in that person's whole history, biology, cultural position, and so on, so as to come as close as we can to erasing any trace of a "decision." If there's something we can't manage to erase, well, there's your decision. Let's move the needle in the opposite direction—let's reconstruct that person's entire "equipage" as completely as possible as a series of decisions, introducing terms indicating alternatives, deliberation, consideration, choice and so on at each point along the way. Let's try and get this act to be nothing but decision—what does it look like then? Where is the non-decision residue? The very fact that we can move from one pole to another in our inquiry suggests, softly commands, that it is better to be able to slide up and down the scale. And what that further means is that the purpose of doing so is to enhance the probability that the subject of our inquiry and all who might model themselves or be modeled on it will be able to do the same—that is, keep broadening the space of decision against what will also be an enlarged background of non-decision. Making more conscious, responsible, aware decisions enlarges rather than shrinks the arena within which decisions are made. So, we have no problem using the word "decision," but we do so in order to name and thereby enact a space of deferral (to decelerate and reverse convergence upon some center), not to create some rules for the proper "scientific" or "philosophical" use of the word.

In this way we show any "decision" to be a result of listening to the center. What I am talking about here is not very different from and, in fact, is an extension of, those occasions where one claims to be speaking in the name of some authoritative entity, and therefore has to distinguish one's own opinion from what one has to say in the name of that entity. So a diplomat speaks for his country, a clergyman in the name of his church, a scholar in the name of the discipline, and teacher in the name of curriculum, a doctor as a bearer of medical expertise, and so on. In many cases, these "delegates" will have prepared scripts or language to work with and professional norms to follow, but there will always be those cases where one reaches the limits of the script, the language, the norms, and one has to decide what one's country, school, profession, church or whatever "wants." This, then, is the model for what we are always already doing anyway, and should therefore do more explicitly and formally. We are always already doing this anyway because there is never a single word out of our mouths that has not been "borrowed" from some "source" we take to be authoritative and which we are therefore helping to further authorize. If any two or more people were to sit down and examine some "specimens" of their opinions on various topics, simply asking each other, non-confrontationally, in good faith and the spirit of inquiry, where all these opinions came from, down to the use of particular words, phrases and grammatical tics, we would see this very quickly. One way of thinking comes from one's parents, another from an impressive teacher in school, another from the media sources one regularly consumes, and so on. Even if each individual could point to specific modifications in these received opinions, those modifications have sources, or the intellectual moves that allowed for those modifications (a certain way of assessing facts or logic) have them. Even the best-read and most scholarly among us would have to point to intellectual traditions and their institutional reproduction upon which we rely and which, like everyone else, we have been unable to fully "vet," right down to the vocabulary and unknown authorities which trail off into the blur of barely recorded or unrecorded history. Everything I am saying here is both obvious, once pointed out, and indisputable, and yet when are peoples' "viewpoints" discussed in this way? Again, the point is not to discredit people by showing their views are not really their own—if that's true for all of us, including those who bring to bear the mechanisms of "discrediting," how could it discredit anyone? The point is that we are all, always, far more "delegates" and "representatives" than we are "individuals," and that formalizing and foregrounding this in social and institutional interactions would provide everyone with more productive ways of contributing to common endeavors. If all these inherited ways of thinking, or idioms, can be examined as ways of "suturing" sites of mistaken uptakes of imperatives from the center, we can also discover ways of improving them, which is to say, of inventing pedagogies.

The kind of inquiry I am proposing be made part of discourse generally would no doubt be vigorous and reminiscent of some early forms of desacralized discourse pioneered in ancient Greece, like "parrhesia" and satire (prophetic explicitness and courageousness as displayed in the Hebrew Bible also provides models). The minimal anthropomorphic vocabulary allows us to first of all identify any utterance as a displacement: if I say something, I make myself a center of attention rather than someone else, and I direct others' attention to some thing in particular, rather than something else. This is true even for the most innocuous or welcome of utterances. There is always a prima facie basis, then, for asserting that an utterance was aimed at that displacement, even has, as its full meaning, effecting that displacement. To point this out is to centralize the other in a potentially violent way while also, of course, leaving oneself open to the identical operation. If this is the mode of entering a discursive space everyone adopts, then that space will be able to endure only under the rigorously maintained conditions. Such an approach to discourse has an undeniable truth to it, while being, under most conditions, unbearably provocative. But the truth can be isolated and the provocation made more bearable insofar as this mode of discourse can be practiced as a discovery procedure. Instead of asking people their opinions, or what they think, which will generally yield a response, even if frank and informative, that minimizes the "usurpationist" dimension of any utterance, one might begin by venturing a hypothesis regarding what they have in fact usurped. The most felicitous response would be to admit to that and/or some other usurpation, and then return the charge, hypothesizing what kind of usurpation might be effected by exposing this one. If everyone is willing to play, we would be mapping out a field of more or less uncertain power, with everyone in a position that more or less coincides with their respective delegations from the center. If we are all usurpers, even if just barely, or just maybe, the only remedy is for each to "deem" the others to belong in the positions they inhabit. So, we have a declarative unmasking ("when you say X you're really doing Y") followed by an ostensive "re-deeming," in order to in-order all. If participants find some instance of usurpation more difficult to redeem than others, that could also be put on the record, also in the name of the center, for future review. What I am modeling here is not a form of government but a more sociable and responsible form of social interaction predicted upon the acceptance of centered ordinality as the originary form of power. If we begin with a secularized admission that we are all out of place, we can further posit that we all might have a place, with the evidence of our belonging in that place to be found in our respective admissions, in the practice of our reciprocal redeeming of those admissions.

Not all social spaces need to be pulled up to this degree of tension—most won't, perhaps, and models can be followed more or less distantly. But the mode of social interaction I am proposing would allow for and demand greater levels of disclosure and honesty, and more controlled and purposeful forms of disclosure and honesty, than anything allowed under liberalism, which must see the usurpationist utterance as the exception and therefore subject to severe censure—however, since no "criteria" for what counts as a real usurpation (or a justified object of resentment) or injustice can be other than arbitrary, the supposedly generous assumption that usurpers are the exception just allows the charge to be leveled at virtually anyone, depending upon the needs of a particular power center. What I am proposing is the possibility that any space can be converted into a disciplinary space in which all the participants are both the subjects and the objects of the inquiry. To assert that someone else is a usurper in his very utterance is to hypothesize a proper allocation of positions that has been disrupted, and what would count as that proper allocation can be read off of the language of "denunciation" itself. It is therefore to pose a problem: how do we identify the boundary line between usurpation and proper occupation? What implications of violent centralization can be found in the supposed usurpation, that would not be found in the proper occupation? Where in the utterance in question can we identify an opportunity for an increment of deferral that went unexploited? Hypothetical utterances that might be seen as being on one side or the other of the boundary depending upon some variable could be constructed. It is in this very process that the participants transition from being usurpers to being, by reciprocal authorization, proper occupants.

XVI

THE AESTHETICS OF THE CENTER

Detecting and articulating boundaries is an aesthetic question. Aesthetics is located on the originary scene, in the oscillation of the attention of the participants between the sign put forth by the other and the object.[1] The desire for the object is magnified when the participant's attention is directed toward it by the gesture of the other; the object then attended to directly is stripped of that desirability, which then has the participant return attention to the sign. What is compelling here, I would say, is the object as presented by the sign: if we imagine this oscillation continuing (which, given the nature of oscillation, we must), with each return of attention to the object some way in which the sign has "glossed" the object remains, eventually leaving the participant with a completed model of the object as marked by the sign, which takes us from aesthetics to sacrality (and then the sparagmos). Sacrality involves representing the gesture as compelled by the object; aesthetics involves discerning the intentions of the center through the attention of others on the scene. This account situates aesthetics on the boundary of both knowledge and the sacred. Knowledge is being able to identify, publicly, two objects, but, really, first of all the same object at different times, or for different participants, as the same. Oscillation between the sign and the object is commanded by the former so as to ensure that all are putting forth the same sign: once this has been ascertained the object can issue imperatives. While we speak of the sign as a ges-

---

1 See *Originary Thinking*, "Originary Esthetics," 119-125.

ture, we should see the gesture of aborted appropriation as the tip of the sign considered more comprehensively, which must include posture as well as gesture: the hand must be mock reaching for the object, but the body must be holding back so as to frame the reach as just a gesture. With each oscillation, more of the body as total sign is encompassed sensually so as to confirm that the sign is the same all around, or determine just how much sameness is necessary to make the judgment.

Like every element of the scene, the aesthetic, over time, is abstracted and brought into new relations to the sacred center. A broader desacralization is necessary before "art" can take on some kind of independence relative to the sacred, but until that point aesthetic considerations would be critical to representations of the sacred. Aesthetics would serve the purpose of introducing, welcoming, drawing participants into the sacred scene, providing ways for those participants to inhabit the scene and minimize the distance between ritual performance and the scene of origin. Participants receive their names from the ritual, which carries the aesthetic dimension into other practices. The separation of art from ritual coincides with the same disruption of sacral kingship that produces politics and the problem of the "tyrant." It's therefore not surprising that central to the first works of art is the problem of the tyrant and usurpation of the center more generally. Both Greek epic and Greek tragedy address resentment toward the usurped center in a direct manner, in an attempt to discover ways in which that resentment might be made socially productive rather than destructive. Art represents the desacralized on the model of the sacred. In modeling the desacralized on the sacred, the desacralized character of the figure will be exposed; at the same time, new forms of attention equipped to in-order the newly opened figure are created—any artwork is therefore more or less consistent in revealing the failed imperative and thereby to replace by replicating the redemption of the center. Gans, in *Originary Thinking*, presents the history of art in terms of whether, and the manner in which, the work of art represents the scene of representation itself. Greek tragedy is a kind of year zero in this regard, as the scene is presented directly, and the audience's participating is mediated directly through the chorus. In other words, no reason has to be provided for why we are concerned with the fate of the central figure or, more precisely, why we share and fear the resentment toward him. He does not need to come into, or be brought to, our attention. Once the centrality of the central figure is no longer a given, the resentment of the central figure himself must propel him to the center—he must be a usurper accusing others of usurpation.

If the central figure must make his way to center stage, he must also be performing for an audience all his own, one he generates and is reciprocally generated by, and that audience must be represented in the work as well. The boundary between the artwork and the audience is therefore represented within the work. The more the central figure is stripped of any supplementary features that make him "inherently" central, the more arbitrary the placement of any figure at the center becomes, and the more interchangeable the central figure and the members of the audience, both represented and actual. Centrality can only be asserted against some other social center, which generates the resentful hero of romanticism, who is subsequently systematically humiliated (made the victim of the audience's resentment) over the course of literary realism. Centrality can be systematically dismantled in the work, in which case the subject of the work is exposing the now discredited means of representing centrality. New figures can be placed at the center, in an attempt to renovate exhausted forms. The boundary between art and audience can itself be placed at the center, in works of art that can only be completed by the reader, or listener. The center here, we could say, is the art "recipient" produced or called forth by attention and devotion to the work itself, a devotion that must be given on faith. The boundary between artist and work, between art and non-art, can also be represented in the work. What we can trace through all of these aesthetic possibilities is a relation to the secular world, all of the energies of which are devoted to discovering ways in which the central figures at all levels can be deemed "non-tyrannical." What kind of unqualified devotion will either evade or redeem the resentment toward the usurper? The secular world is comprised of the vast archipelago of disciplines, springing originally from philosophy but also politics and the circulation of money. All of these disciplines are in service to power, including the more narrowly scientific and technological, and their respective objects of study are the myriad forms of super-sovereignty that might remove, at least temporarily, the stain of tyranny from social institutions. Means of discipline aimed at organizing our attention in certain ways toward certain kinds of objects are presented as legitimate by the disciplines because they are dictated by some anthropomorphic model that renders that means of discipline in accordance with nature, the authority which can't be superseded. Knowledge depends upon aesthetics: only a center free of usurpationist desires can sustain attention on the gap in imperatives issued by the center, and only aesthetic oscillation can dissolve those desires into the manifold forms of attention directed toward that center. But the disciplines must present themselves as prior to the aesthetic because their secularized, object-centered forms of knowledge cannot see the discipline as a scene. This means that the relation between the work of art and the disciplines is satirical: all secular art is a satire of the disciplines. (If it's not, then it's not art, but rather promotional material for the disciplines.)

All satire needs to know is that someone else could be at the center other than the one presently occupying it—and that is always the case. Of course, the same is true of any alternative occupant of the center proposed by figures on the margin, and it's true of whatever power center must be occupied in order to effectively propose an alternative. Satire is effectively total, and includes itself. Satire sees everyone as aspirants for some center who fail to see the inessentiality of that aspiration, which is to say, its roots in mimetic desire and resentment. Such a view of others can be discerned within the aesthetic moment on the originary scene itself: part of the oscillation between sign and object on the scene is a recursively articulated representation of one's fellow signers. Running up to the issuance of the sign each member sees his fellows as dangerous—it is fear, not just of physical harm (although very much that as well) but of the collapse of order that leads into the presentation of the sign. Once others have signed, though, they must also fear, and oneself must also be dangerous. What does the other look like, riven by extreme vulnerability and projecting a threat, all in one instance? I think we have our answer if we think about what is perhaps the most typical figure of satire: the blustering bully whose pretensions are easily punctured. Satire is the most pedagogical artistic form, because if we are all capable of seeing one another (and ourselves) in these terms (which is not to say we should always and only see each other in these terms) it will be a great aid in preventing the escalation of resentments: much more so than seeing ourselves and others as tragic heroes, romantic victims, or lyrical soloists, all of which leave residues of resentment once centrality has been demythified and which therefore call for renewed sacrifices. (It is also the case that learning always proceeds through a series of satires, in which the boundary between voluntary and involuntary can never be completely certain to either, on the part of the learner toward the teacher.)

Originary satire, then, which is also a very portable aesthetic form, is the manner in which we can carry out the discovery procedure initiated by representing each other as usurpers of whatever position we all occupy by virtue of our utterances. Increasingly proficient satirical performances will situate the respective usurpations within the various disciplinary scenes which enable one or another usurpation—the psychological, sociological, legal, economic, and so on concepts represent means of ascendancy within a given setting while also being the means of demonstrating the limits of those pretensions. Without originary satire, one can't really get anywhere close to an understanding of the disciplinary social order that would allow one to act in any way other than as a puppet of some power center or another. Satire is not infinitely sustainable itself, though—successive and reciprocal representations of others as uniting the extremes of threat and vulnerability reduce those extremes, and one can proceed to obey the imperative to enter scenes of imperative mistakenness and resolve the gap between imperative given and imperative obeyed. Now, though, it becomes possible to stand before the center by treating the disciplines not as imperative frames demanding your obedience to a super-sovereign composed of resentment toward the gesture toward any mode of sacrality (center-directed sociality), but as semiotic materials comprising a scene upon which we can see ourselves participating in resolving the imperative gap. We can know that we know in the name of the center.

The secular disciplines all share the same origin: the elevation of the declarative sentence to the primary linguistic form, in accord with the metalanguage of literacy. This doesn't free disciplinary practices from ostensives and imperatives; rather, it generates imperatives and ostensives out of the declarative order itself. The declarative commands you to withdraw some demand and convert it into an interrogative—declarative sentences are always answers to at least one of at least two possible questions (one concerning the topic, one concerning the comment). The imperative of the declarative order is that questions need to come from some uncertainty regarding imperatives or ostensives generated by a previous declarative. Any declarative sentence can be checked for meaning and reference: can whatever it posits doing whatever it is doing in fact do that thing; can we find our way toward possible ostensives in the world (and scenes anchoring those ostensives) that would make the declarative an answer to a question? If the declarative (and in speech act terms, the constative) is the primary, and the ostensives and imperatives (performatives) are the derivative forms of speech, there shouldn't be any imperatives or ostensives that can't be derived from a declarative—imperatives and ostensives are merely implementations of the abstract model of the declarative, which must descend into reality due to some contingency. We should really, eventually, with the help of algorithms and computers, be able to dispense with imperatives and ostensives altogether and generate a complete declarative model of reality that would account for all possible ostensives. Any secular discipline must construct and defend the integrity of its own space by ensuring that this is indeed the case—that there are no stray imperatives or ostensives that the declarative order would be secondary to. This involves establishing and enforcing rules for proper imperatives and ostensives ("proofs"). This is the source of the super-sovereignty that has involved the disciplines in a millennia-long struggle with central authority, which must issue imperatives before they have been "justified" on terms that would be satisfactory to any self-maintaining discipline.

That this is the unspoken imperative of the discipline—that the prerogative of the central authority must be usurped and represented as derivative of the discipline—is the starting point of secular satire. Whatever, within the discipline, is represented as the result of an impeccable string of declarative sentences can be represented satirically as resting upon an ungrounded command. The disciplines themselves must incessantly issue commands that they have not themselves "sufficiently" justified through their own metalanguages, and since the disciplines cannot allow for this possibility they are more "tyrannical" than any central authority. The discipline creates concepts meant to apply to its object of study, while the discipline also maintains its immunity to those corrosive concepts, which situate the "object" of study as dominated by some mythical order from which the discipline is to liberate them. The secular satire applies the concepts of the discipline to the discipline itself, creating an "infra" disciplinary space within the discipline wherein the anomalies generated by unauthorized imperatives and ostensives can be enacted and examined. Satire brings an irremediable, incorrigible mistakenness into the discipline, enriching the declarative order through both convolutions and simplifications, precisely by acknowledging the primacy of the ostensive-imperative world. The ostensive-imperative world permeates the declarative order—in making that statement its author commands you to identify the traces of that world in these and other sentences, and to treat the constitution of the boundary between imperative and declarative as an event, in which declarative constructs make present previously unnoted imperatives in their own predecessor sentences.

Satire is the most mimetic of the artistic forms—often an exact reproduction of an act or utterance, in a slightly changed context, is enough to expose the imperative embedded in the declarative. (Indeed, a mark of strong satire is that one is hard-pressed to distinguish original from copy, with the only difference being that we see and say about the latter what we ignore or remain silent about in the former.) And it doesn't take a lot to modify declaratives into imperatives in such a way as to show, as Alasdair McIntyre has pointed out,[2] that the descriptive and explanatory concepts and norms developed by the modern human sciences depend on, are bound up with, and provide instruction to, the institutions and practices that shape the behaviors and the subjects those discourses purport to account for. To characterize the human subject as a "rational decision maker," for example, is to abstract that subject from its embeddedness in institutions and traditions and see and respond to only those behaviors that correspond to the model of "rational decision maker." The same goes for char-

2 In his *After Virtue*.

acterizations of individuals as consumers, voters, workers and all the other categories that place individuals and groups external to each other, to themselves, and to any form of centered ordinality, subjecting them to the mode of super-sovereignty making the designation. To describe me as a consumer is to command me to consume, and if I make explicit that command I can, in turn, if provided with the necessary pedagogical resources, represent the world back to my designators as containing nothing but objects of consumption that I chow down compulsively like a Pac-Man. That would, really, just be me hearing your description as an order and implicating you, through my obedience, in the order you have summoned into being. In which case, are you quite sure you want to describe us all as "consumers"? (What do participants in the discipline, as participants in the discipline, consume?) Satire is a great purgative: whatever survives it might be able to last. And there's always a very simple way to get started: imagine what the difference would be if a particular declarative sentence came from one source rather than another, or in answer to one question rather than another. Originary satire minimizes by representing all the boundaries constitutive of the work of art—between art work and audience, art and non-art, artist and work—so as to make a separate art scene unnecessary while therefore even more abruptly interrupting other scenes like traveling players emitted from the center.

XVII

MEDIATED
CENTRALITY

We can see the different speech forms as different media, even in the sense that each can be used to channel the others in revealing ways: you can point at something in order to ask a question about it in some contexts, a question can really be a statement, a declarative sentence an obvious, and ominous, command, and so on. Whatever marks an utterance as one form or another, or some overlapping of forms, is what marks it as media, because the simplest way of thinking about media is as whatever provides for the scene enabling and constituted by the sign itself. The first medium is the mimetic structure of the originary scene itself, with the symmetry spread across the scene and mirrored and modulated from one body to the others setting the stage for the gesture of deferral. We can take this tightly organized network, with each "station" "pinging" the others, as the model for all media. Mimetic theory is usually too quick to find its way to easily recognizable examples of imitation, like those found in the mimetic triangles of desire so critical to René Girard. Marcel Jousse's "mimism," though, reminds us that mimesis, or miming, works on much more levels both more fractal and more macro, and continues operating within the "ideas" and "social structures" that we can take to be moderating responses to mimetically generated violence.[1]

---

1 The collection of Jousse's writings edited by Edward Sienaert entitled *In Search of Coherence: Introducing Marcel Jousse's Anthropology of Mimism* is most important for my use of Jousse here, but I'll also be drawing on other recently re-issued volumes, *The Oral Style* and *Memory, Memorization and Memorizers*.

For Jousse, every move we make is not only mimed, but recalls and deploys ("revivifies") all the muscular and other physiological responses deposited in the "anthropos" from previous mimings. The world and any knowledge we have of it is mimed, not in "images" in our "minds," but in our bodily movements, stillnesses, and tensions. As soon as we come into the world we orient ourselves to our surroundings by miming everything in it, with our eyes, ears and touch. With our mimed gestures, we act back on the world, forcing new disclosures on its part, which we mime in turn. All our communications and interactions with others are saturated with miming, something which is easy enough to notice if you look at the eye contact, nodding, head tilting, word repeating and checking, body opening and closing that is evident in every interpersonal encounter. Jousse insists that even more technologically advanced and abstracted forms of media, like reading or films, are thoroughly mediated mimologically. How have we attained the control over our body that allows us to sit still, face forward, eyes focused on black print on white page, as we read? Even this non-movement is miming, as we would probably confirm if we can remember the days of learning to sit quietly over books and other reading materials in schools. On the originary scene we should imagine a cumulative reciprocal matching of body parts and movements as part of what we call the "gesture of aborted appropriation"—as I've pointed out, any stray movement, any sudden move within the process of "lining up" in front of the object could easily lead to the breakdown of the scene. Jousse is necessary for anthropomorphics because he doesn't remark on the causal primacy of miming and then go on to talk about the activities we already have familiar names for, like "religion," "art" and so on. He insists that we focus on the constitutive mimological character of each and every one of these human endeavors.

It's extremely instructive to consider that one's attempt to construct a complex string of arguments, aimed at displacing and modifying some other complex string of arguments, is riddled throughout with the oral and written styles derived from the rhythms of vocabulary, grammatical constructs, habits of paragraphing and punctuating, assonance and alliteration, and so on, which one has mimed from others and now inhabits as a result of an entire lifetime of reconstructing and recombining these rhythms. Even more, the fundamental purpose of the clichés, formulas and parallelisms Jousse identifies in the oral style, that is, memorization, is no less central to our mimetic and pedagogical practices to this day. It's true that we don't need to memorize actual texts, but more tacitly we have to remember learned responses to texts, to conversations, to questions, to implicit and explicit imperatives, to a world of emergent ostensives—if we look closely, we can see people's self-centerings organized through various mnemotechnic devices that involve remembering who they are. In other words, we have to remember the scenic forms of our interactions with others. Jousse believed that we have abstracted or "algebrized" ourselves away from our native miming spontaneity by giving ourselves over not only to writing but mathematized forms of social interaction (which corresponds to what I would call a hyper-declarative order), but he provides us with ways of seeing an equally pervasive miming being carried over into these media as well. The reason we are more than just a jumble of dissociated mimes inscribed in us through the billions of separate "events" we live through is because we bring the mimes that "stick" into various rhythmic relations with each other; and eventually into what Jousse calls "style," or the becoming conscious of the mimes working their way through us. ("Becoming conscious" would simply be a higher order miming involving imitating ways of controlling and coordinating gestures and utterances.) Jousse's project is a profoundly anti-metaphysical one, which would have us recover our rhythmic birthright, and which has formed a crucial tributary into the study of the difference between orality and literacy pioneered by Millman Parry's study of Homer, continued by Alfred Lord, Eric Havelock, Walter Ong, of course Marshal McLuhan, and others—a tradition which I have taken David Olson's more recent work to be a kind of culmination of. What Jousse does not consider is the problem of violence, or mimetic rivalry, viewing the gestural world as a kind of Eden which has never really been lost even if it's under threat in certain more "educated" regions of the Western world. It's not surprising, then, that even though Jousse would seem to be especially well placed to hypothesize regarding the origin of language he, on the contrary, considers it to be a non-problem, with oral language itself simply a form of gesturing, making use of a different combination of muscular networks—those producing sounds that originally just supplemented gestures. How we could have ever gotten lost in the algebraic modern world then seems to be a problem, but I have no interest in engaging in a "critique" of Jousse here—like other seminal thinkers one has to accept that what he can give you may very well depend upon him not being able to give what he can't.

And what Jousse, resituated within originary grammar, can give us is a model of originary media, which subsequent media progressively distance themselves from, retrieve and supplement. In other words, I am suggesting a more general application for Olson's reference to "classical prose" to illustrate the operations of the metalanguage of literacy. Let's say that the "media" is whatever makes a scene hold together as a scene, and whatever makes it hold together as a scene is whatever provides a space for the sign to signify. This provides us with a kind of continuum for articulating scene and sign: we can see the sign as a minimal "protuberance" on a densely networked or mediated scene; or, we can see the sign maximally, as requiring an extensive articulation requiring only a few "props"; or anywhere in between. To use Gregory Bateson's definition of "information," the sign is the difference that makes a difference on the scene, and any judgment on what counts as this "difference" can only be made from within another (disciplinary) scene. So, originary media is a network, a set of invisible lines we could hypothetically draw connecting the sensorium of each of the scene's participants to each other's, but also to all the different "parts" (what counts as a "part" depends on the vision, embedded in a body in motion or stasis) of all the others' bodies. We would even have to draw lines directly from body parts of one participant to body parts of others, as we should assume tacit, tactile and subtle forms of responsiveness on everyone's part. So, just as the metalanguage of literacy supplements whatever on the speech scene that cannot be directly represented in writing, everything "horizontal" in the originary media would have to be supplemented in subsequent scenic articulations; and, just as classical prose generates the simulation of a scene upon which the author and reader stand with the topic of the prose, all subsequent media aim at an equivalent simulation of those lines connecting us bodily to our fellow participants.

Just like the sign is immersed in the scene without there being any definite boundary separating them, the scene itself is immersed in its surroundings, making its surroundings conditions of its own scenicity. To follow up on the previous discussion of aesthetics, every medium represents itself as a medium in its distinction from the surroundings it converts into its conditions—again, without any definite boundaries. An early human ritual maximizes everything remembered to be present in the first ritual, with such memory itself being a series of mimings, supplementations and simulations—everyone is dressed as the animal placed at the center, everyone has a prescribed part in the drama represented in the ritual—all this is media. This mediated scene closes itself off from whatever isn't the scene—the forest beyond the clearing where the ritual takes place, say. But if there are noises from the forest, or an animal appears from it, the community will likely be able to respond to such contingencies from within the ritual, giving these new additions a part, using them to further substantiate the scene. They may become serendipitous additions to the established ritual. But this would also mean that members of the community are attuned to what is non-scene as potential scene, including other animals, water, sky, sun, stars, and so on—all of which could become media insofar as any of it can be brought in to supplement the scene and more precisely distinguish the sign. This is all miming—if the wind, for example, becomes medium by blowing through the ritual and modifying the setting of the ritual, this is because the effects of the wind can now be mimed, but if those effects can now be mimed, that means they were always already mimed, which would explain how they could have been imagined as contributing to the ritual in the first place.

Anthropomorphic immersion in media follows from the insistence on "attentionality" as the basic, and, strictly speaking, only category of thinking needed. From attention to the center, the entire scene is taken in, including everyone else's attention to the center. We don't even need to introduce concepts like "intention" or "will"—it is prolonged, distributed, and returned attention that itself accounts for bodily movements toward the center and postures and gestures framing and positioning the others on the scene. If you look at another closely enough, imitating his gestures is part of that attending, and if you along with others pay sustained attention to an object, the manipulation of that object and the practice of pointing to different parts and aspects of it is also nothing more than a more continuous, patient and engaged form of attention. The guarantee of mutual understanding is both parties being able to point to the same thing, at the same time, and to point to each other pointing; everything we call "media" are means of holding, shifting and directing attention, across space and over time. It is through sustained attention that we solicit and record the imperatives coming from them, and seek out links in the chain of imperatives going back to the originary call to defer appropriation (at the very least, the thing you're looking at is telling you to keep looking)—which means that the best way to understand what someone is doing, and why, is to identify that which commands their attention.

I'm not going to get into a detailed analysis of the tremendous developments in media over the last century and a half that have had the effect, most obviously, of enabling simultaneity over great distances—unlimited simultaneity across the planet, in fact. I will just point out that what the model I've just constructed would suggest must be seen as a problem each form of media—radio, TV, film, the internet, etc.—must solve: how to draw those horizontal lines connecting all the participants in these very different kinds of scenes. What kinds of miming, supplementation and simulations allow for the operation of these different media? Already with writing, we have a medium that constitutes not a single scene, but unlimited possible scenes. In what sense is, say, a modern translation or performance of *Oedipus Rex* the "same" as the one first read or performed by Athenian citizens? This is a way of asking in what sense we are on the same scene as those Athenians. Insofar as we are, that shared scenic relation is generated mediatically: through histories of performance, transmission, study, translation, and so on—all of which are forms of media generating signs that go into the composition of a transhistorical scene, a present, upon which that text or performance might be the "same." So, those horizontal lines are drawn by reaching into the surroundings of a given media and incorporating some of those surroundings into the media. Now, the miming, supplementations and simulations I have been contending are constitutive of the media are also the elements of the media that "critical" media theorists have always taken to be sources of mystification. Isn't it, after all, the illusion of believing in the lovers' passion on screen, of participating in the woes of the novelistic character, that enables one to be "interpellated" by the "dominant ideology"? In other words, the media generate the illusion of all whose attention it draws being on the same scene. It's not just an illusion, but it's that as well, and a potent one insofar as the devices employed to generate the experience of sharing a scene conceal the historic mediations that actually make the scene the same in a different sense. New scenes can then be generated to represent the mechanisms used to generate the illusion. Paying attention to the scene, bringing the scene and scenically transformed elements of the non-scene into the sign is all part of the practice of originary satire—we could say this all involves enhancing our resources as mimers beyond what the current media would, strictly speaking, allow. The challenge is to develop modes of inscription that uncompromisingly expose the historicity of any particular scene (including the scene of inscription itself) while inscribing a transhistorical (anthropomorphic) model of exposure that persists through the successive scenes organized around the text. But we can now pursue all these inquiries without that other illusion of laying bare, once and for all, an unjust hierarchy to be dismantled in the creation of a just egalitarian order. It is remarkable that almost nobody really believes in such a transformation while at the same time everybody does, as is evident from the omnipresent references to "examining power relations" and the still popular gesture of muckraking into "abuses of power," hidden "power elites," and so on. Yes, there are power relations, and abuses of power, but no power-free or power-neutral model against which to measure them. No one wants to say what, exactly, "non-abusive" power would look like because then they'd be confessing that power hierarchies can in fact be unobjectionable—that is, virtually no one can think outside of the opposition between the tyrant and the holy victim. What could be more illusory than that?

The dominant medium today is the internet which, as Eric Gans has pointed out,[2] tends to assimilate all other media to itself: here, we see the work of miming, supplementation and simulation of one medium with regard to another taking place. But the inter-

2   "On the One Medium," in Cowdell, Fleming and Hodge, ed.

net is itself modeled on a rather ancient medium: the archive—books, themselves a kind of medium, placed in a single location (another medium), catalogued in various ways (more media), used by those specially trained to do so (more media—more miming, supplementation and simulation). The internet is an all-inclusive and immediately accessible archive, and it makes all signs, scenes and events instantly archivable. Archives were used to collect all the relevant cultural products of a civilization; the internet archives everything indiscriminately. Relations between elements in the archive are determined by algorithms abstracted from searches by users and shaping future searches. So, if you search "Charles Dickens Bleak House" you'll get connected to critical discussions of the novel, Dickens's other novels, novelists contemporary with Dickens, like Thackeray, Chancery Court, the all-consuming civil court that a subplot in the novel is centered on—in what proportions would depend upon what readers, critics and scholars focus on in their studies of the novel. The internet distributes scenes of inquiry which overlap with each other in varying degrees. What doesn't come up in searches will eventually disappear from the culture, even if in principle it will always be there to be retrieved. The algorithm is a supplementary medium for this more abstracted, distributed and immense archive in process.

The primary form of cultural activity is therefore becoming archival work (we're becoming curators). We're always constructing "portfolios," in which one cultural item we take to be significant is shown to be significant because it adds to the significance of other cultural items. And part of what makes an item significant is that others have asserted its significance. Social and cultural theories are essentially models for conducting searches and building relationships within the archives so as to construct hierarchies of significance. Sometimes we'll assert the significance of something as lying precisely in the refusal of others to grant it significance. Anyone who has spent much time on blogs outside of the "mainstream" is well aware of how pretty much every dominant narrative of the 20th century West is currently under extreme strain, and it's not clear how much of the Whig history that has reigned supreme over the past 70 years will remain intact. All this is a result of archival work, and a lot of it simply involves juxtaposing texts that have been made central alongside equally (or more) compelling accounts that have been "memory-holed." It wouldn't be too much of an exaggeration to say that's all that Mencius Moldbug did in constructing his political formalism. It's with far less exaggeration all Moldbug's opposite, Noam Chomsky, did, well before the internet, in his political writing ("here's what the *New York Times* says; here's what this paper in Managua, or Beirut, or Madrid says…").

Media as archive suggests a way to begin thinking about alternative and counter-models of education, at all levels. Instead of packaging and delivering standard narratives as the school system does now, just have students, from the beginning, charting pathways through the archives. Have students juxtapose multiple narratives around a single event or historical figure, using different media from different periods and from different perspectives. Have them keep noticing differences between the narratives, and building profiles of those narratives. These would be scenes of inquiry that are in turn deposited back into the archive. Teachers can be there to help out and ensure students construct sufficiently challenging projects. Learning how to read and write would be part of this process—dictionaries, grammar, rhetoric, logic and other resources are also part of the archives. This approach would break up ideological commonplaces and cultural monopolies, while organizing everyone around the process of inquiry itself. Of course, the possibility of such a pedagogy depends upon the coherence of power, which itself depends upon the mimological relations between different levels of power: the coherence of power would be measured by the extent to which we see mimisms articulated through the various chains of command comprising the social order: do those with more power model practices that subordinates can, in turn, analyze and replicate in ways that are later incorporated by the commanders? This inquiry would yield far more valuable information than those predicated upon liberal notions of consent, dialogue, communication, shared beliefs, sympathy, solidarity and so on. Can we actually show an institution to be engaged in a shared project? And do all institutions participate in shared projects modeled by the central authority? These would be the properly pedagogical questions.

Knowing is being able to say, see, these two things are the same or, even more radically, that this thing is the same as itself. Naming something confers identity over time, but over time differences pervade what has been named and doubt enters whether we are indeed talking about the same thing. The preservation of names clearly can't be carried out by ignoring, suppressing or denying these differences. Rather, it involves restoring or renaming by identifying what makes the thing the same in the wake of and as a result of all the differences that have entered. This means you have to be able to say all the ways it is not the same, not even the same as itself, for all the people who would contest its identity; and then say it is the same for everyone insofar as they can set aside all those differences as part of the medium or background against which the thing can be presented as the same. A thing can only be the same as a center of attention resulting from a lowered threshold of significance granted by a sustaining center. In that case, listening to the center is following this thread of the same, of the name, on a scene peopled by those obeying the imperative to shed from the name whatever has been compromised by difference and must be relegated to the background, or made medium. Pedagogy is the provision of a gesture, a mimeme, a chunk of language, a construction that can be kept the same precisely by articulating it with innumerable other gestures, mimemes, chunks and constructions across media and time. You know it is the same insofar as you can transmit it to others who can keep it the same even across wider fields of differences.

XVIII

CENTER
AND DISTRIBUTION

The proximal cause of the breakage and spillage of the sacral order is money and capital. For secular theory, labor, property, money, the market and capital are the real underpinnings—the "structure"—over which "cultural" and "political" institutions are superstructured. Within these secularized frames, all agents are external to each other, which means they are most fundamentally opposed to each other, making the primary theoretical question how do they ever manage to cooperate? Starting with the center, as both occupied and signifying, reverses this approach. Now we can see all these concepts as the results of delegations on the part of central authority, and of efforts to extend that authority, to overcome limits to it, and to restore authority once those attempts to overcome limits have produced competing power centers striving to influence or occupy the center. Markets do not spring up spontaneously out of an evolving division of labor, leading to the use of currency to ease the growing scale of transactions, and then to debt and capital as a result of the unequal success experienced by the various players on the market. Markets are created by states so as to provision their militaries when abroad, and money is supplied so as to enable soldiers to participate in those markets. Debt is originally used to dispossess farmers as the state or more powerful landowners encroach upon their possessions.[1] Modern capital is the power to abstract individuals, groups and perhaps most importantly of all, entire disciplines, from the traditions and

---

1 Graeber's *Debt: The First 5,000 Years* is crucial to this discussion.

communities within which they are embedded so as to introduce them into new hierarchies. Power is ontologically prior to and causative of, markets and all the rest.

Markets are real insofar as they are what people without direct authority for maintaining the social center do with knowledge, information and skills when they are being protected and bounded but not directly supervised by such authorities. If the central authority assigns to a member of the ruling class the project of producing a certain number of vehicles in a certain time, he will not need nor want a thorough account of all the decisions made by the individual receiving the delegation. Nor will the individual receiving the delegation want such a complete account from those to whom he delegates. Everyone has a sphere of power and command, and expects those under his authority to find ways to cooperate so as to meet the demand. Since "total" supervision is impossible, since there will always be some space between an imperative given and one obeyed, attempts at total supervision are signs of a dysfunctional power order, one riven by power struggles in which each attempts to attain the mantle of super-sovereignty. In a functional power order, no more power is given or sought than that needed to complete the assignment. The people working at the middle and lower levels of a social order, then, will be involved in various exchanges and, insofar as forms of cooperation are sustained and institutionalized, might very well end up interacting in ways suggested by liberal economic theories. The fact that corporations need to be chartered by the state, which could in principle revoke any charter once the corporation ceases to serve its declared primary function, means that the primacy of the state over economic agencies is already conceded, even in liberal societies. Indeed, the prodigious technological developments of modern Western societies owes far more to its enduring corporate structure than to more recent inventions like liberalism and democracy.

The center distributes. The carcass on the originary scene distributes itself, or is distributed among the participants by the presiding and enduring being of the victim, as pieces to be consumed. The earliest forms of distribution are just such divisions of food items, no doubt matched, more or less roughly, with contributions made to the center. This is a gift economy, or what I have been calling "imperative exchange," which can be widely expanded to include relations between families and clans. In the case of conquest, distribution takes the form of what Carl Schmitt called the "Nomos," an originary division of land among the participants in the conquest, no doubt proportional to their respective contributions and the command hierarchy. Distribution can later take the form of grants of titles and rights to make use of one's property in various ways. The establishment of towns organized around artisans, guilds and markets, with specific rights, tied to specific obligations, for all, is yet another kind of distribution. The introduction of money into these settings is yet another distribution, aimed at modifying the effects of the other ones. If we think of the center as the source of distribution and, also, as the effect of its distributions, we will never be able to imagine it makes sense to think of rights without corresponding obligations—the nexus of rights and obligation, the imperative exchange, is simply what distribution from the center entails. This would be true on local levels as well. Peasants would want more land, guilds would want tighter protections, merchants would want greater latitude in their dealings—that is, authority would be tested. But the tests and questions would be meaningful in relation to the founding nomos and the traditions it generated. Let's say that the model of imperative exchange must have reached its limits in the feudal order in a manner similar to the conditions I hypothesized earlier regarding the ancient imperial order. It may seem obvious that this must lead to the "freeing" of all subjects from all fixed reciprocal obligations such as has been effected by the modern liberal order. But if what follows imperative exchange is not merely negative freedoms, but interrogative imperativity, that is, the question of how to devote oneself completely to the signifying center, then the answer lies in new forms of the nomos, providing access to the invisible to create new and more minimal hierarchies.

The introduction of money to empower those more directly dependent upon the ruler indicates some lack of security of central authority—it means indirect forms of power, rather than formalized, direct ones, have become necessary. There might be measures that can be taken by the central authority to control the supply of money in such a way as to recoup that power deficiency, but the more social interaction is mediated monetarily the more likely it is that the state itself becomes monetized. The problem here is that the state needs masses of people mobilized for various projects, and to mobilize them they must be abstracted from their embedments. For the state to directly initiate such abstractions is to risk generating opposition from various power centers—only by recruiting those power centers themselves could the central authority reduce the risk sufficiently. It's easier to recruit power centers that are themselves already abstracted and thrive on abstraction—risk takers, who can be integrated or dispensed with as necessary. In that case, those abstracters must be permitted to make demands of the central authority, which is to say abstract its own modes of performance. The other approach to abstraction, and the only one consistent with central authority, is the assignation of teams, directly accountable to the central authority, with the authority to take whatever measures are necessary to improve the functioning of the institution. In other words, the form of institutional innovation proper to secure central authority is "skunkworks," or teams empowered to work outside of established protocols in order to accomplish specific tasks. This is a fractal form of centered ordinality, and provides the basis for permanent forms of rule, insofar as the central authority can always "seed" skunkworking teams, announced or unannounced, within institutions so as to keep attention centered on the primary institutional function. In this way, the originary social form is retrieved in a way that counters the tendency of formal delegation to create inscrutable forms of power that resist further formalization.

The traditionalist opposes abstraction in the name of full embedment, but the possibility of rejecting abstraction disappeared with the rise of divine kingship a few millennia ago. By now, the forms of embedment defended against abstraction are the results of previous abstractions that have been re-embedded. The question is, in what form will abstraction proceed? Or, what kinds of mobilizations are necessary? If the market operates within the capillaries of the system of supervision, then abstractions should contribute to that system. The paradox of power is that the more central the authority, the more authority depends upon the widest distribution of the means to recognize authority; to put it in grammatical terms, the paradox of power is the paradox of the most unequivocal imperative leaving the largest scope of implementation of that imperative. As Andrew Bartlett explains very thoroughly in his aforementioned "Originary Science, Originary Memory: Frankenstein and the Problem of Modern Science," abstraction always involves some desacralization or, to put it more provocatively, some sacrilege. Sacrilege can be justified on the grounds that the innovation it introduced will enable new forms of observance of the founding imperatives of the social order. So, the sacrilege should be, as Bartlett argues, "minimal," while the new forms of observance (I depart from Bartlett's formulation here) should be maximal. Abstraction creates new "elements," and therefore new relations between elements. Monetary and capitalist abstractions are pulverizing, creating new elements that are identical to each other, and therefore most easily mobilized for any purpose. This is the process of "de-skilling," with its ultimate telos being automation, that labor theorists have known of for a very long time. Any mode of abstraction consistent with secure central authority, or autocracy, meanwhile, would make ever finer distinctions between skills, competencies and forms of authority within disciplinary spaces. In this way, abstraction carries with it its own form of re-embedment.

The market economy, then, becomes a measure of fluctuations around the threshold at which the paradox of power is made explicit. Let's imagine a king turning himself into the largest property owner in the realm, and formalizing, as disposable private property, all that is possessed at different levels of authority within the kingdom. The king converts much of the army into his private security force, and the rest are distributed to the various lords, barons, merchants, and so on. Let's further assume some external market every producer within the kingdom can sell to, which would in turn create internal markets. Let's also accept the libertarian assumption of a consensual legal system, which settles contractual disputes and violations of property rights. The community would be converted into a mass of competitive enterprises. Some would do better in the competition, and would put the less successful out of business, buy up the pieces and equipment of failed companies, hire the former owners, and so on. The trend would be toward a hierarchy of monopolies, in which case supply chains could be agreed upon by the companies themselves. The real purpose of establishing a market is to break up one system of distribution and create another. In our example, the market would cancel itself, and we would end up with what is essentially a single company supplying all of the society's needs, unless the more powerful monopolies undertook to introduce competition at the lower levels in order to provide themselves with a wider range of available products and workers. But once this process is initiated, the different leading monopolies would end up in competition with each other, as the new companies they form or break off out of existing smaller ones would serve one monopolistic concern better than others. The more competition, the more instability and insecurity, the more collusion and counter-collusion, the more fully marketized and monetized the social order: it is only at this point that prices are again needed in order to determine which producers are creating more value for the community. Now, that point at which the leading monopolies would intervene in the smaller ones is the point at which a central authority could behave in exactly the same way, and undermine itself in order to have more direct access to its materials; or, the central authority would act directly on the emergent mismatch between formal designations and actual functioning by inserting teams into the relevant companies on the model I suggested above. In this latter case, the paradox of power is made fully explicit: all members of the social order are following the imperative to richly implement the imperatives issued by the center; in the former case, the paradox of power is obscured: explicit power is a mask for hidden and unaccountable forms of power.

All social conflicts can't be reduced to this fluctuation, but all social conflicts are "processed" through it. This is most obviously the case for everything grouped under the concept of globalization, most especially movements of capital (at the "high" end), especially financial, and migration (at the "low" end). Globalization represents a raising of the threshold at which the paradox of power is made explicit: global corporations have been released from obligations to any central authority and construct their own command chains, which include governments as subordinate partners; advocates of increased migration exercise power across borders that national states find it difficult to counter. In both cases, states are set up so that they must respond to the same "market" incentives as the corporations and migrants themselves. This is the case even if globalization is an imperialist strategy advanced by one or more leading powers—in that case, the new powers ceded to subordinates end up compromising and colonizing the home government itself. That government (or those governments) might even become more powerful in terms of the effects they can have globally, while still becoming less powerful in terms of their ability to control or even predict those effects. We could imagine a point at which the paradox of power would take on an inverted form, in which it becomes explicit that central authorities would not be issuing "operational" commands at all—commands would just be one more incentive (or disincentive) agents further down in the chain of command would have to take into account by assessing the likelihood of any penalty for disobedience. Of course, this is already regularly the case, as corporations weigh the costs and benefits of possibly paying a fine for breaking some law or regulation as opposed to losing whatever advantage on the market the transgression provides them.

Within a market order, then, any action, event or relationship is characterized by a fundamental duality. On one side, however thinly, the paradox of power is in play: all actors recognize that their sphere of activity is protected by some more powerful agency and constrain and direct their activity accordingly. On the other side, to some extent, imperatives are converted into market signals—that is, a site of exchange where one person's power to punish or reward you must be balanced against lots of other peoples' power to do so. In both cases we find an interaction between center and periphery—in the first case, one acts in a way that redounds to the authority of the center, thereby creating space for the further replacement of external by auto-supervision; in the second case, one tries to subject the central authority to incentives and disincentives similar to the ones we are all subject to—this ranges from simple bribery and other forms of corruption to the vast avenues of influences made legal and even encouraged within a liberal social order, like lobbying, forming interest groups, political donations, think tanks, media propaganda and so on. We could locate anything anyone does, thinks or says somewhere along this continuum and study social dysfunctions accordingly.

Probably the most intuitively obvious argument in favor of the "free market" is the Hayekian claim that all the knowledge required to carry out production and cooperation at all the different social levels is far too distributed and complex to be centralized and subordinated to a single agent. This is of course true, but also a non-sequitur and a distraction. A general must provide some leeway to his subordinates, and they to theirs, and so on, and for the same reason—the general can't know exactly what this specific platoon might have to do under unexpected circumstances, and he can't even know all that one would need to in order to prepare them for those circumstances. There will therefore be "markets" all along the line, as people instructed to work together to address some exigency organize "exchanges" of knowledge, skills and actions amongst themselves in order to do so. The general doesn't need to know $1/1,000^{th}$ of all the specifics of these interactions to still be the general—that is, to issue commands that can be obeyed, and to place himself in a position to ensure that they will be. The same is true for those institutions charged with providing communications, health care, education, transportation, housing and so on. In each case, capillaries along the margins of these institutions can be adjusted in accord with the level of responsibility to be allowed consistent with meeting the purpose of the institution. The argument for markets is really saying no more than that you can't do a very good job if you're being micromanaged at every point along the way. It's equally true that you can't do a very good job if the terms of each move you make have to be "negotiated" with a constantly changing range of agents.

Liberalism has generated the illusion that what appears below the threshold of direct supervision is what, in fact, determines the form of supervision; even more, that the supervision is a servant of those actors which have merely been provided some leeway. This situation produces destructive delusions, because the presumably free agents are nevertheless aware of their utter dependence upon their "servants." Is there any businessman who thinks he would be able to protect himself against violence, fraud, robbery and extortion by those readier than him to use violence and break laws without the force of the state? No businessman believes this, but in a way they all believe it, because their political theory leads them to assume that, first, there were a bunch of individuals engaged in peaceful exchange with each other and then, only when criminals and invaders, presumably attracted by the wealth thereby created, tried to take it using force, was the state "hired" as a kind of Pinkerton to maintain order. This makes it impossible to think coherently about the simplest things, such as how a policy everyone would recognize to be beneficial might be conceived and implemented in the best way.

XIX

CENTERED
TECHNOLOGY

In large part this book is a critique of (strategy for entering and transforming) the secular disciplines. The project, or imperative, implicit here is to roll back the power circulation that takes the form of equalizing abstractions (whether of money or votes) into abstractions conducted by formalized and explicit power hierarchies. I've been suggesting that rolling back money and votes is conceivable—if one considers, for example, how much of market activity is mediated by informal networks among agents who have been authorized by some form of power, it is easy to imagine minimizing the effects of market signals on economic activity— indeed, it's possible to imagine abolishing economic activity in itself, and "incorporating" corporations as one kind of institution among many others within a well governed social order. The same is not true of the most thoroughgoing form of desacralizing social practice, and the most socially central: technology. To review: insofar as power is desacralized, there is nothing but mutually hostile "interests" engaged in struggle over the decaying corpse of the social body; at the same time, power is never genuinely desacralized, because as soon as the sacred center is punctured, mythicized centers like "the common good," "the voice of the people," "Constitution," "rule of law," and, eventually, "GDP" are set up as masks of what everyone must assume is there—an unquestioned authority rooted in a singular origin. These mythicized centers are intrinsically arbitrary and divisive, though, which means they must eventually escalate hostilities into some "total" form.

Desacralization of power, though, is possible because there is a difference between the ritual center and activities engaged in outside the center. In the earliest human communities, we can assume that in activities apart from the ritual center nothing at all changed after the originary event, while the ritual center was made to reproduce as precisely as possible the originary event. But the sign deployed on the originary scene, along with the constraining structure of ritual, would be extended to other activities; at the same time, linguistic development towards the declarative would involve the attribution of actions to ("mythical") occupants of the center. The mythical interpretations of ritual would be drawn from the far less interesting but nevertheless determinative actions outside the central aura and be converted, ritually and mythically, into actions modeling behaviors for the community. Out in the field, hunters battle their prey; on the narrativized ritual scene, the sacred beast/ancestor battles with its family and enemies, takes pity on humans and gives life to the group.

As social cooperation increases, stories of the origin of each new mode of cooperation would be "heard" or derived from the center—no member of the community could do or create something new without attributing the discovery to a mythical agent. You would in turn be obliged to that mythical agent, and would give to it some part of the fruits of your labor, which in turn would be part of the individual's contribution to the center for the entire community. (The center remains the center insofar as it distributes.) The gift the god has given you comes with an imperative: in one form or another, that imperative would be to use it in such a way as to honor the donor. In return, the individual issues an imperative to the mythical being: a prayer, requesting aid in successfully using the skill or implement. All the implements of work and war would be created within this frame of what I have been calling an "imperative exchange."

The implements themselves, their parts, and the implements used to produce the implements, are themselves all part of this imperative exchange. This is to say there is a "magical" component to the process: ritual words and gestures must be applied to all acts involving production and use, and instances of successful or failed use would implicate the implements themselves, which don't simply break, and aren't simply poorly used, but refuse, for reasons that may be more or less formulated, to follow the commands given them. In a certain sense we could say that, of course, an early human smoothing out his spear knows that this has to be done so that it can fly straight and fast when thrown, but his way of thinking about it will be framed completely in terms of being in harmony with all the agencies of the surrounding world mediating its production. Such processes become institutionalized, and to craft some item in a way that is not traditionally prescribed and monitored by the upholders of that tradition would also be unthinkable.

So, the question is, how did it become possible for "technology" to emerge—that is, production conducted outside of these forms, in accord with the logic of continually reducing the elements of one process to another set of elements produced by another process? I think that the answer must be: when it becomes possible to see other human beings as implements. The divine kings, commanding hundreds of thousands, even millions, in their slave war and labor armies, made up of the socially dead, would first get a view of all these individuals as "parts" of a whole that might be more than the sum of its parts. Some could be added; some subtracted; some moved over here; some over there. If some worked harder, the possibility of combining all the better workers would come to mind; if workers or soldiers improvised and found some new way of cooperating with each other, that could be remembered and reproduced. This is already a kind of technology.[1]

The Axial Age acquisitions of metaphysics and scripture facilitated the collapse of the ancient empires that could readily levy these vast, sacrificial, masses. So, in the European middle ages, while there was steady technical development, and some remarkable feats of engineering and architecture, such development never exceeded the limits set by existing corporate and authority relations. The masses confronted in the New World, then in conquered regions abroad and, finally, those at home flowing into

---

1 Lewis Mumford's work, like *Technics and Civilization* and *The Myth of the Machine*, inform these reflections. More recent, and contemporary, work, based on the presupposition that humans are co-constituted by their tools and machines, will also be informing this discussion—I'll just mention Yuk Hui, whose *On the Existence of Digital Objects* and *Recursivity and Contingency* synthesize the thought of Bernard Stiegler, Gilbert Simondon and others within a broader post-phenomenological framework; and Benjamin Bratton, whose *The Stack* and *The Terraforming* I'll be addressing later.

the cities from the farmers enclosed out of their land must have ignited a new technological imagination. For quite a while, the development of machinery seemed to track pretty closely intensifications in the division of labor, with each laborer being given increasingly simpler tasks within an increasingly complex process, with those tasks eventually being transferred to technology. If automation has now itself become an autonomous process, it is because men were first automated. Eventually, of course, technology came to alleviate and eliminate human labor, but in the process the disciplines, focused on both technological and human resources, became the main drivers of social development. The human sciences, which took over from theology and philosophy, treat humans in technological terms, as composed of parts that work together in ways that can be studied and modified. Even attempts to "humanize" disciplines like psychology reduce people to sets of interchangeable and predictable clichés.

The disciplines naturally think they should run the government which, after all, is just another technology. And whatever claims the government might make on its own behalf, like fulfilling the "popular will," are best left to the disciplines, upon whom the government would anyway be dependent in measuring such things. The emergence of data and algorithm driven, all-intrusive social media which more and more people simply can't live without is a logical extension of this process, as is the elimination of millions of jobs through new modes of automation. But desacralized technology, like desacralized power, provides a frame within which ultimately unlimited struggles ensue. Indeed, technology is the dominant form of power. If technology presents itself to us as an enormous system of interlocking imperatives which provides a very precise slot for us to insert our own imperatives, who or what is at the center? What ostensive sign generates the system of imperatives?[2]

2 Benjamin Bratton, a contemporary thinker informed but not restricted by postmodern thought, and refreshingly free of humanist and liberal sentimentality and cant (and a barely concealed disdain for leftist posturing), uses "climate change" as what Dan Hill in his *Dark Matter and Trojan Horses: A Strategic Design Vocabulary* could (but probably wouldn't) call a "MacGuffin" to introduce the possibility of a totalizing recentering of institutional organization. Bratton poses the question of whether new forms of power will be needed so as to "repurpose" technology properly; or, on the contrary, whether the restructuring of power rela-

Technology is completely bound up with the specific forms the centralization of power takes in the wake of the desacralization of power. It is part of the same furious whirlpool of decentralization, as old forms of power, predicated upon earlier forms of technology, are broken up, and then recentralization, as new forms of power exploit the new technologies to remove mediating power centers in zeroing in on each individual. In that case, the commands of the center are mediated technologically, which is to say through our self-centerings as both objects of technological manipulations and imaginings and subjects becoming signs of the algorithmic paradoxes: our choice here is to become either predictable and unreliable, or unpredictable and reliable; that is, either try and fit the categories comprehending us and become as defective as those categories; or, extract and improve upon the imperative embedded in those categories. In the latter case, we situate ourselves at the origin of the technological event, and model forms of power that will advance participation in the reinscription of technological markings upon us.

The telos of technology, then, is to make technologically produced human interactions into models for further analysis of practices into networks of sub-practices, out of which new practices are synthesized. In the process, the cultural work of deferral becomes increasingly technological—this means that we will think more in terms of deferring possible conflicts in advance, in making them unthinkable and impossible, rather than intervening crudely after the fact. We would work on turning binaries into aggregated probabilities, and making those aggregated probabilities capable of expression in language—this would be a source of important artistic and pedagogical projects: finding ways to express aggregated probabilities in language would mean populating the future by hypothetically placing centrally ordered teams at various posts where new practices will be required. It would be as if we were producing futurity by continuing to work on the originary scene itself—in, say, settling "in advance" some dispute between friends, a particular wrinkle in the fluctuations of aborted gestures on the scene is revealed—the scene, one can

tions can best be conducted indirectly through technological innovation. Bratton favors the latter possibility, while I would favor the former, but I would agree this is a good way of posing the question.

now see, would only have cohered if one member had shaped his sign of deferral while positioning himself just so in relation to his neighbor and the center.

What about all the moral and ethical questions bound up with technology—gene manipulation, increasingly destructive weapons, pharmaceutical interventions into behaviors, deficiencies and capabilities that were once within the normal range but now, at a higher resolution, seem to call for remediation, etc.? Behind all these anxieties is the fading away of a sense of the human that was formed logocentrically, which is to say through the assimilation of the literate subject to the scene of speech, in which all are present to each other, and intentions are inseparable from signs. Humanism is a degenerate form of the Axial Age acquisitions. But this is not to say that our telos as technological beings is simply to go full speed ahead on all counts. We need a new way to think about these things, one that doesn't rely on what are ultimately historically bound feelings of defilement. There is a human origin, and origins that iterate that origin, but no human nature (unless one wants to call "orientation to the center" a "nature"). The event of technology, in which we become, collectively, models of further interventions that will in-form us, is itself anthropomorphic.

Some of those moral and ethical questions are not real questions, relying on dumbed down or falsified versions of actual or possible scientific developments. The answers to those of them that are real questions will depend upon the state of the disciplines. Only within disciplinary spaces will it be possible to ask whether a proposed innovation or line of inquiry, i.e., some proposed new power, will have commensurate responsibilities assigned to it. Only in properly composed disciplines can these questions be raised free of scapegoating pressures demanding remediation to enjoy new "freedoms" or to avoid some form of ostracism. Anthropomorphically grounded disciplines would have to work to make new innovations and inquiries consistent with the basic terms of social coherence, while using new possibilities to continue studying those terms; and then we would have to assume open channels between the disciplines and central authority. There is even a place for "letting the market decide," as long as we keep in mind what the "market" is: what people without direct authority for maintaining the social center do with

knowledge, information and skills when they are being protected and bounded but not directly supervised by such authorities.
Supervision can be relaxed and tightened for various purposes,
and one of the purposes for relaxation is certainly to see what intelligent and talented people can do when encouraged to engage
in skunkworks. In this case, as in all cases, the ultimate test for
the reception of any novelty would be whether it helps sustain
the pyramid of command starting from the central authority, and
even contributes to ensuring the continuity of that authority from
ruler to ruler. Will a particular innovation make imperatives from
the center both more unified, coherent and simple in proportion
to the scope it provides for authorities at lower posts to enhance
and complete those commands in obeying them? And the disciplines will, accordingly, make themselves over into articulations
of practices refined by the latest divisions in labor that study the
diverse forms of human interaction for models of technological
transformation—in the process establishing meta-practices for
representing this dialectic in a way intelligible to central authority. Each individual could think of himself as both an operator of
technological forms and a model for future ones, but the latter
only in proportion to the former.

Capital and technology come to represent independent forms
of power because they are levied by the occupant of central authority against other potential contenders for central authority
and thereby become independent sources of power. This has to
be addressed on a geo-political scale, because capital and technology are exported and imported and this process involves competition between sovereigns regarding the control of what we
would have to call vassal states. It might seem to follow from the
claim that all human activity derives and answers to a singular
center that the entire world eventually needs to be brought under a single government. I think the more coherent assumption
is that the world needs a formalized hierarchy of powers. This
keeps us close to actual global structures, which are comprised of
states of various levels of independence and sovereignty. Insofar
as the international order is organized in terms of independent,
nominally equal, states, the maintenance of hegemonies in the
form of asymmetrical alliances and spheres of influence must
be conducted largely indirectly. If a more powerful state wants

to prevent a less powerful state from breaking a chain of vassal states required to maintain regular economic or political relationships, it can refuse it loans, stop buying its exports, accuse it of human rights abuses calling for cutting off aid, and so on. These actions require the cooperation institutionalized in banks, trade agreements, international courts, human rights organizations, the media (to propagate the required narrative), and so on. This disorder, in turn, encourages rival powers to play the same games, or different games reflecting different power positions, economic, cultural and military means of projecting power. These conflicts generate ideologies which feed back into the system. Short of world government, rivalries between major powers will always be possible (since I'm not going to explore the possibility of world government here, I'm not going to address the issues of what kinds of rivalries the attempt to establish it might promote). The purpose of formalized power is to concentrate relationships in responsible institutional heads; what this implies for world order is government to government communications, with no support for oppositional or subversive movements within another country— at the very least, this means that disagreements between major powers will result from genuine, substantive conflicts of interest which are in principle negotiable, rather than from proxy conflicts and reciprocal projections spiraling out of control. Since it seems highly unlikely that the two or three major powers will be identical in power, we can assume a single world hegemon, whose power in relation to subordinate power centers we could think of by analogy to a national sovereign governing an array of local institutions: the more unhindered and explicit the exercise of power, the less intrusive it needs to be. Only under such conditions could the flows of capital be brought under political control, and reduced to the relation between the central authority and the world of the disciplines, in which conditional grants of authority matched with commensurate access to resources are monitored by skunkworking and potential skunkworking teams reporting to the central authority.

XX

TURNINGS TO THE CENTER

"Alienation" is a word that hasn't really gone out of style. It seems to apply just as well to today's labor conditions, people's relations to unresponsive, even hostile governments, the desiccation and depravation of culture, deteriorating relations between the sexes, as it ever did. But if we're alienated, what are we alienated from? Critiques of alienation, whether coming from Marxism, existentialism or new schools of psychology presupposed some natural or ideal condition from which one was alienated—some intuitive sense of wholeness, from which the splitting of the subject against itself was a deviation to be remedied. So far, I can say that we are alienated from our proper relation to the center. Our secular condition, and its entire vocabulary, which can only define the world itself against a demythified center, perpetually refilled with disposable scapegoats, can only define all the agents in this world in opposition to each other—even the individual or subject can only be defined in opposition to itself. Everyone's externality to each other is a useful way to think about alienation. All anyone can do is invoke some super-sovereignty that the state "should" be "accountable" to and deploy it against their opponents. More precise than (and complementary to) "alienation" might be another term that has been straddling the boundary separating pop from disciplinary culture for decades: "meaninglessness." "Meaninglessness" can be treated quite literally: a lack of access to the center takes the form of words not having any determinate meaning. We can work with the cliché of, say watching TV as a meaningless activity, and this can lead us to delve earnestly into the empty soul of the TV watcher; or, we can ask what the word "watch" means, and whether this meaning can be redeemed when applied to viewing TV—if no, then the real problem is in our language, not our souls (and it's easier to think of tending to our language). Anthropomorphic inquiry as establishing the meaning of words retrieves something fundamental to the reification of declarative culture in literacy, which first of all made it possible to speak of "meaning," a central concern in the earliest philosophical texts. Words as the sites of thought experiments identifying the boundaries distinguishing them from other words; words as originating in ostensive-imperative-declarative articulations; words as subjected to the disciplines; words as mistakenly conscripted into new uses: inquiries along all these lines are part of the anthropomorphic project of restoring meaning. What we want above all is to mean what we say. If there are subversions in the background of our discourse that empty our words of meaning, we would like to remedy that. David Olson shows that literacy introduces the distinction between "speaker's meaning" and "sentence meaning"[1] (by delegating to the reporter of speech the responsibility for supplementing the conditions enabling and attending the original utterance), and once we have such a distinction the latter can get away from the former, which means one's words are at the mercy of all the ways in which they can be repeated in different contexts. Clearly, the solution here is not to install a kind of homuncular simulation of the author in texts to ensure they don't stray from the speaker's meaning; rather, we keep returning to our words as they are returned to us, supplying them with more explicit ostensive-imperative articulations that were only tacit the first time around. Others can continue this project after us, as they come to inhabit our words and take on the same stake in ensuring their meaning. As Michael Polanyi has contended,[2] we know more than we can say; for this very reason, when what we say is handed over to other forms of knowledge, we have to make what we have said sites of shared knowing we contribute to along with others.

According to Thomas Kuhn's theory of scientific revolution, pursuing the questions generated by normal scientific activity leads to the discovery of more and more facts that cannot be rec-

1 *The Mind on Paper*, 101.
2 *The Tacit Dimension*.

onciled with the regnant theory that determines the relationship between observed facts. These anomalous facts are, through increasingly complicated means, made consistent with the theory, until we get to the point where accounting for those anomalies requires the proposal of new theories, one of which will eventually institute a scientific "revolution" and thereby initiate a new period of normal science. However that may be for the physical sciences, in the human sciences we need a different model of disciplinary transformation. In the human sciences, it's the meaning of "key words" within the disciplines that become anomalous, and eventually take on new meanings. Anna Wierzbicka's work is rich in examples of such transformations (her study of the change in the meaning of the Anglo legal term "reasonable doubt" in *Experience, Evidence and Sense* is exemplary) and Google's ngram viewer provides us with the somewhat different but closely related phenomenon of new and transformed words creating new regions of reference in real time. If we abjure the use of some metalanguage that might put all this linguistic movement in order, the only way of working to make knowledge out of linguistic evolutions is by entering different linguistic domains and signifying from within them. At first glance, of course, the teeming new vocabulary of, say, transgenderism, can be seen as a transparently partisan attempt to hijack the language in the ongoing wars of the cultural left against normal sexuality, the nuclear family, gender difference as experienced by the vast majority of the population, and so on. This perspective is accurate enough as far as it goes, and there may be times when some new linguistic field can be "waited out" or successfully resisted in the name of some existing and still powerful vocabulary. In general, though, it will always be possible, and it is more generally the more powerful strategy, to enter such linguistic fields and supply meaning to its terms where they are lacking. Whenever possible, new linguistic fields, whatever their origins, should be redeemed—not in the interest of compromise or dialogue, but of knowledge, which can only be generated by enriching rather than restricting linguistic potential. There are many ways of making anomalous linguistic fields consistent with existing ones: any decentering can be treated as a search for the center. Key terms of contemporary liberalism, like "racism," "sexism," "homophobia," "transphobia," "Islamophobia," and so on, will best be reworked from within, rather than resisted from without, or simply turned against the original users (such as accusing the anti-racists as being the "real racists"). Yes, "racist," in its most common uses, including those uses the newly accused are nostalgic for, is just liberalism's equivalent of "counter-revolutionary"; but lingering over the term, and making explicit the full range of by no means internally consistent phenomena it brings into view is what will eventually both de-toxify the term and use it to notice new things about what we notice in our attempts to figure out what the center wants from us. We may almost be at the point where accusations of racism have so proliferated that it will be incumbent even upon "anti-racists" to ask what, exactly, makes a particular statement or gesture "racist"—the results should be interesting. (Almost any systemic description of reality carried out under the banner of anti-racism can be redescribed, perhaps more systematically and sustainably, in radically different terms.) Working on saying what we mean can involve clarifying and simplifying what we say, and bringing our practices into accord with common, or more consistently excavated usage; but it can also mean finding ways to mean a lot more things.

XXI

THE END OF SECULAR
THINKING

I suggested above that the exemplary secular subject is the usurper—from everyone's perspective, everyone else is in a position they wrongly occupy. This is a condition of universal resentment—open, seething, constant resentment directed against the false center that has allowed some other to occupy one's own rightful position. But this is the condition of all secular thought, and without a unanimously acknowledged center, any other mode of thought would be sheer fantasy. The world of usurpers at least provides us with recognizable agents, actions, motives, struggles and causes: we can understand why one would want to usurp, why one would want to usurp a usurper, how the specificities of one's usurpation or counter-usurpation would singularize one, how alliances, divisions of labor and various forms of cooperation can emerge among those defending their usurpations. The very fact that I have distilled secular thought to a world of usurpers even though, to my knowledge, no actual secular thinker has ever used such a description, demonstrates the generativity of secular thought. Secular thinkers have thought in terms of rulers, and various justifications for rule and obedience; about social groups in conflict, and "just" or "pragmatic" ways of resolving those conflicts; about individuals, and their "rights" which they can claim against other individuals and the state; about competing and contradictory interests, and so on. If we say that all that can motivate all these agents is resentment, as the naturalness necessarily attributed to them is an after the fact attribution produced by the attempt to reconcile the conflicts they engage in, that reduces to a world of usurpers. At best one could achieve a stance of comic detachment—but what is that, other than a kind of shadowing of one usurper after another? And this would make mimetic theory, and originary thinking as the highest form of mimetic theory, the end of secular thought, as it brings us to the universal condition of usurpers who now, perhaps, can see why others see them as the usurpers. The configuration of the originary scene strips bare all the "reasons" we have for our resentments to the mimetic rivalry directed toward and restrained by a center. (No doubt many of the reasons we have for our resentments are good ones—some, at least, must be better than others—but that would still leave open the question, why do we resent—as animals do not—even when we have "reasons"? Why can we hardly ever say anything that is not some articulation of resentment with a grudging concession to the center?) The next step, then, is to move beyond secular thought.

Doing so involves exhausting secular thought, bringing its paradoxes to their conclusion. Secular thought depends upon the liberation of the declarative order from the ostensive-imperative world. The declarative sentence produces a linguistic present that does not depend upon ostensive presence. The declarative sentence does this by projecting possible ostensive presents to which the participants in the declarative event are ready to attest. If I say that someone is "not here," in response to a request that they be made available, my claim has meaning on the condition that the person in question has been named and noted, that my interlocutors have been made aware at however many degrees of separation of this naming and noting, that there is some "somewhere else" where someone else could be attesting to the presence of this person, that there are people who could attest to the attesting, bring word of it to me, and so on. Further inquiries could be made at any point along any of these chains—if it is a fictional representation, then all these possibilities are being modeled, and maybe the very process of modeling is being modeled. So, the declarative generates rather than removes itself from the ostensive-imperative world. Even supposedly meaningless ("colorless green ideas sleep furiously") and sample ("the cat is on the mat") sentences serve to construct a disciplinary present, in which we deliberately "subtract" meaning and context so as to direct attention to, say, the purely syntactic dimension of the sentence. But the fact that the declarative sentence generates a multitude of other possible presents, the "failure" of any of which would lead to the collapse of the present constructed by the declarative sentence producing it, represents a paradox for the sentence—whatever it asserts both is and is not—and, therefore, a crisis. There does, after all, have to be a present of the utterance, even if the sentence itself can only refer to that present by making its reliance upon the present of some "recipient" of the sentence explicit.

By "present" I mean not anything philosophical, but the present tense, which is the first and, I want to suggest, only, real tense. Other tenses are modeled on the present tense—grammatical inflections indicating tenses are ways of showing there are other present tenses that can be represented within the linguistic present of the utterance. Imagine if we spoke only in the present tense—rather than saying, for example, that "the Declaration of Independence was signed in 1776," we would have to refer to a field of presently existing documentation recording, and recording the recording, and registering the consequences currently noticeable, of the signing of the Declaration of Independence in 1776. The past event would have to be nominalized into a nounphrase, while mentioning it today would have to be formalized as mediated by a range of presently available references, evidence, and "traces" across the culture. We'd be referring, not to an event that happened and is done with, but to a field generated by and radiating from an event we know only through that field. Here, the paradox of the declarative, that it dissipates its own present in the articulation of it, would be made explicit and formalized, and in the process the grounding of the declarative order in the ostensive-imperative world would be made present.

In this case, the representation of successions of events, fully "tensed," is mythical. Saying that something happened yesterday is mythical because it's still happening today. To close an event in its own present is to make the center of that event a site of imperative exchange, which is to say it's sacrificial: whoever paid for that event is whom we owe in return. We can't pay debts to the preceding generations, but that's because we are present with them, as they mediate for us the imperatives we receive from the center. So, if we are Americans, the imperative transmitted by the American founders to rebel against "tyranny," in the name of "natural rights," is still an imperative for us to work out, even if we scrutinize the specific claims made in the Declaration and find them wanting, even if we determine the revolution was really a self-interested move by an alliance of farming, merchant and banking elites enabled by anti-monarchical elements in Great Britain, even if we conclude it was merely a convenient justification for maintaining and continuing slavery, intensifying the expropriation of the native inhabitants, and so on. The ostensives gathered in all these other references bring with them other imperatives which we can make part of the declarative order through which we resolve the imperative mistakenness conferred upon us by the existing institutional structure of the United States. We could easily say, "the United States is the real tyranny," against which we must rebel in the name of some other configuration of "natural" or "human" rights, and so on; but the harder question is to determine where the central authority lies within the United States, as best we can approximate it, how we can identify the imperatives coming from that at least partially hypothetical central authority, how to obey those imperatives in such a way as to make that central authority more central and more authoritative, and so on. If we accept the pastness of those historical narratives, they pull us in incompatible directions, obligate us to competing imperatives; if we treat them as present in their effects, they become commentaries on the imperatives we obey now. In the end, we'd have to be able to say that the only real meaning of "rebel against tyranny in the name of natural rights" is to clarify for us a history of commands that precedes and succeeds that one. A good start on constructing a more comprehensive and consistent field of imperatives might be to note the curiosity of the framers of the Constitution modeling the office of the president on the only man they could imagine occupying it first, George Washington. Why could the construction of this new form of republic only be completed only once such a position and its occupant could be so precisely imagined? That imperative to construct a new form of post-monarchical, post-sacral, central authority can still be retrieved and obeyed: what remains is to generate the historical narratives showing how this imperative, elevated, best provides consistency to all the others.

I'm not calling for "banning" other tenses than the present (even if the proposition to do so is a very useful thought experiment) any more than I was, earlier, calling for banning the use of psychological terms like "decision." There is a method at work here to display and displace linguistic and historical accretions and supplementations. Things do "happen," and people do "do" things. For that matter, people "say" things, and the things they say can be "true" or "not true." I can assert all this confidently not as a result of a line of philosophical inquiry but because Anna Wierzbicka shows that every language has these words, and I accept the unanimous verdict of humanity regarding them. "Someone can do something" according to the primes, which means all languages can account for the "possible," which is to say another present "extractable" from the present. Of course, none of the nominalized terms we take to be virtually synonymous with the verbs (if we can say something is true, can't we call that statement the "truth"; if we say someone can, can't we say they are "able"?) are in the primes. These words, like the tenses, are supplementations and simulations. Again, this doesn't make them "false"—just sites of disciplinary inquiry. Methods deriving from the primes, as I suggested above, would bring into focus the relation between saying someone "can" and someone "does," someone "thinks" and someone "says," someone "feels" and someone "knows," and so on. But most elemental might be the relation between "do" and "happen," because any event can be represented as someone doing something or as something happening to someone, and displaying the difference between the two would make the event or "happening" fully present. It's not as if one cancels the other: if you represent someone as having everything happen to him, you can then turn around and represent the same event as being completely of his doing, precisely by having his doing "marking" the happening.

Instead of getting bogged down in arguments over the real causes of events (biological, social, cultural, political, economic, historical, etc.), we would then be amplifying the present, where traces of all kinds of causes can be identified on the spreading field of the present. This implies a disciplinary space aimed at making present a pedagogy of the present. A more precise answer to the question, "what are we alienated from" is "a pedagogy of the present." There can't really be a more fundamental human relation than pedagogy, and firstness on the originary scene and thereafter is really a pedagogical relation; even more, a linguistic pedagogy relation. Pedagogy is fractally hierarchical: the most egalitarian group you can imagine will be broken up, in the daily and minute interactions between its members, into pedagogical relations in which one member teaches another something else that the first may know simply because he got to that place seconds earlier. The origins of trust and faith in each other lie in such pedagogical relations: these relations are formalized by the earliest human groups as rites of initiation. The most systematically and permanently hierarchical group relies equally on pedagogy— it just stretches out the pedagogical relation (what is entailed in "learning" something) over longer periods of time. "Teach" and "learn" both come from words meaning, simply, point out a way to go, on the one hand, and follow that way, on the other. Pedagogy can also, of course, range from minimal to maximal (answering a question; years-long initiation), from tacit to explicit (modeling performance; providing detailed instructions), and so on. One way or another, this is all we're ever really doing. Part of my purpose in introducing Marcel Jousse in my earlier discussion of media was to get to the point where we can think in terms of the fully "mimological" pedagogy Jousse himself calls for, in which we continually construct practices that help us see the social origins of our practices. We could think of it as follows: every act we perform, every word we speak, every thought we have is a result of vast layers of imitation, of which we are aware to widely varying degrees. Any single gesture could be analytically dismantled into wide, "horizontally" transmitted "versions" made available to anyone of us with differing degrees of force; and, "vertically," or temporally, as any gesture rests upon convergent and conflicting vectors of tradition. Stumbling blocks to human cooperation lie in the ways these unthought and unfigured layers of mimetic modeling generate rivalries which, in turn, cannot be represented and therefore deferred. Allowing gestures to unfold "inappropriately" makes it possible to demonstrate where the gesture is proceeding automatically, regardless of a present field of desire and resentment. What has been tacit can be made explicit by modeling the inappropriate act from within the present scene. Sometimes its inappropriateness may be made visible; sometimes it may be rendered appropriate through a generous representation. Either way, something new is added to the repertoire of human practice as blind, almost automatic mimetic modeling is represented and converted into explicit reciprocal modeling of one another. Anthropological and historical inquiries into the origins of the displayed gestures create new disciplinary spaces, further refining the repertoire. Since both micro- and collective practices can be modeled, pedagogy is the means by which higher order practices can be imagined. Everything tacit which is made explicit can in turn be analyzed, automatized, and articulated.

If this is what we're doing all the time, how can we be alienated from it? Well, there's doing, and there's doing. A pedagogical relation is effective insofar as it's embedded in some centered ordinality. A declarative order alienated from the ostensive-imperative world (that insists on having all imperatives and ostensives generated declaratively) disallows the formation of sustained embedment within centered ordinality. This is because the more independent the declarative order, the more it would have you learn from those justifying the practice rather than those performing it. The imperatives coming from the declarative order are primarily prohibitory and hortatory: from "don't treat other members this way," or "don't use too much of this material" (imperatives derived from legal, political and supply-chain considerations) to "respect others in your group," "be a team player," "be accountable to your subordinates," i.e., imperatives that are universally applicable and therefore universally irrelevant. Nothing like "do this, this way, now," can ever come from the alienated declarative order—the declarative order, in itself, is hysterically antagonistic to that kind of imperative relationship (almost any "do this, this way, now," can be interdicted under some reading of "don't treat others X way"). And such an imperative relationship is central to any pedagogy. Even on a more intellectual level, telling a student to "write clearly, provide reasons for your arguments, refute counter-arguments," etc., is meaningless and even abusive, because these admonitions cannot carry with them the criteria for determining when one is actually doing things this way, or coming closer to doing things this way; only a command to imitate a model, and then look, together, at how the model has been imitated, how it can further be imitated, and what habits need to be changed so as to imitate more perfectly (and out of which arise more abstract questions like "what counts as an imitation under changed conditions?") can enact a non-alienated pedagogy. With a model to refer to, utterances and gestures are read as forms of resentment (a desire to displace another); while a pedagogical relation to the model is read off of the resentment—the more detailed the examination of the resentment, the more intricate the pedagogical practices it discloses. The other has stolen from you, gone behind your back, taken your place when you were otherwise occupied; that other has made a demonstration regarding your dependence on your goods, your vulnerabilities, your networks of trust, your assumptions of order in the world; it may turn out in the end that stealing, double-dealing and dispossession is not exactly, or not only, what happened. At any rate, there will now be contributions to the securing of institutions of trust, verification, interdependence and ordering that you will be able to make.

Within any declarative sentence there is a hypothetical centered ordinality waiting to be enacted pedagogically. You stake your place in the expanded present of the declarative. Any past tense opens the question of the reception of that past; any future tense raises questions regarding how one imagines the doings and happenings projected being populated. The same for aspect and mood—they all construct presents in which people are doing things, seeing things, saying things to others who in are turn converted into those positioned in some relation to maybe doing things or having things happen to them. There are virtually unlimited positions open in any sentence that one might occupy. And you're not a usurper if you're in another's sentence. If someone says it's going to rain tomorrow, that someone has heard a forecast from some source that has been made available through some medium, and has some reason for trusting that source enough to let your trust in him be put to the test by providing this information—there are people, working with technology and media, at each point along the line here. If you're not at the head of the line, you are taking orders from another and passing them on, and how and why you do that is your pedagogical accountability. If you're being given information, you're being asked to do something with it, to make some difference, maybe in your own practice, maybe in that of others. The information comes with an imperative embedded in it, in other words. Maybe you're within the order that's transmitting that information as good; maybe you're in another order that treats that information as bad, or questionable, or as providing some meta-information about the sender—in that case, it has another imperative embedded in it. How you enact this part, obey this imperative, is your pedagogy. The centered ordinality you are most directly embedded in is, in its turn, embedded in another centered ordinality of which you are more or less directly aware, which your immediate center wants you to be more or less cognizant of. You need to refer to that higher order insofar as there are inconsistencies in the imperatives directed at you from your immediate center. How you formulate those inconsistent imperatives into interrogatives that can then be "transposed" onto some declaratives that exhaust or "evaporate" it is also your pedagogy. Increasing pedagogical positions within centered ordinalities is the way the declarative order is disalienated. What we all really want is to know that we can do things with others in ways that, because of those ways of doing, things happen that we see happen because of the things we do.

A completely "pedagogized" order, then (everything anyone does can be described as an effect of a network of pedagogical acts), abolishes secular discourse. It does so without any need for a specific sacred order, or form of transcendence. It contains the residue of secular discourse, though, which means it also retains the trace of the sacred within the significant. Once the possibility of seeing all subjects as usurpers in relation to each other (and therefore themselves) has been grasped, it can't be forgotten: we must incorporate this basic human possibility, which has enabled us to construct the very originary scene that accounts for it, into whatever order we create as a remedy. The ever present possibility of the charge of usurper being directed at another, even in the most indirect or implicit ways; that is, the possibility of centralizing violence, is the originary event of an order immune to secular thought. The trace of the sacred in the significant is in the "leap" into a new order involved in the act of naming. The target of converging violence is named as the thing not adequately portrayed or described in the incitement directed toward it. We name in the name of the occupant of the center, the central authority, who is in fact the most likely and common target of incitement, the most vulnerable to charges of usurpation. A mature order would realize that any call for the removal of the occupant of the center must be false—that is, the occupant of the center is not the one to be removed for such and such a collection of reasons. To name is to commemorate: here, we defended the center against this subversion. And when other members are violently centralized, those members and the time and place where that violent centralization was arrested and reversed, are also named, as other points where a subversion of the center, this time less direct, was averted. Naming is also the most basic pedagogical act: nothing better marks the minimal hierarchy self-evident and modeled in any pedagogical act than saying "we'll call this _____"

Naming is the result of pedagogical practices of solicitation of the center. As usurping subjects, we want things from the center; we make demands. Everything we want is really a demand from the center. This means we all have what we could call a "central imaginary": a proto-narrative of the center as the agent that could meet our demands. One side demands that the state protect the rights of the unborn; the other side demands it protect the rights of women to abort. What both sides agree on is that the state should be able do whatever the one making the demand would want: a state incapable of enforcing laws against abortion would also be incapable of enforcing laws allowing abortion. So, the state needs, at least to be capable. So, what makes the state capable? Or, more precisely, what interferes with its capability? If, by whatever historically evolved process a particular social order has for placing individuals in the position of sovereign, once someone is in that position, that person is unable to perform in the way mandated (the way he promised his voters, his party, or those who appointed him through whatever mechanism), then making demands of him is pointless. So, all our competing demands on the state can be deferred in the name of inquiring into what kind of state could do the kinds of things we are asking in the way we are asking. Could a state that operates the way ours does perform in accord with the expectations implicit in the demands we make on it? (So, for example, certainly the contemporary American state could raise the minimum wage to \$20 nationwide if it set its mind to it; could it, though, hold everything else in the economy and society constant so that raising the minimum wage would have the precise effect those demanding it want?) Such an inquiry would reveal at least some of the demands to be inoperable; even more, it might reveal that the very mechanisms by which demands are generated, circulated through the system and used as feedback by the sovereign, guarantee that those demands will not be met in the "spirit" in which they are made. Just laying bare all our resentful, usurpationist demands would reveal, in increasingly rich institutional detail, that the kind of central authority that could meet our demands in a way we could recognize would also be a central authority that could and probably should ignore those demands while instituting more workable forms of feedback. Made more intelligent thereby, even the citizens of the existing social order could intimate transitions from that order by providing "audits" of institutional forms that both provoke and frustrate inoperable demands. In the end, we'd replace our demands with better ways of following commands.

An onomastic pedagogy commemorates and honors sites and figures marking the arresting of violent centralization, but operates far more broadly insofar as we remember that a declarative sentence named the God who abolished sacrificial imperative exchange and that the declarative sentence can therefore be taken up as a form of naming as well. Mistakenness in the imperative chain appears; a gap is opened between an imperative issued and the one to be obeyed; linguistic presence is threatened. Only a declarative capable of generating new ostensives can resolve such a crisis, and the path to the declarative is through the interrogative. That is, first of all, a question must be formed out of the impasse of the imperative. Let's put it bluntly: everyone was depending upon you to carry out a task within a chain of command upon which the rest of that chain depended, and you screwed up. Everyone is angry with you, and demands follow quickly: you should be replaced, you should be punished, you should be supervised more closely, you should be demoted, etc. Well, maybe any or all of that will turn out to be appropriate, but then there are other questions: how singular was this particular task? How singular did it turn out to be, compared to what might have been expected? Whose responsibility was it to vet, train, and prepare you? Who is available to replace you, and how quickly? And so on. These are all predictable, "mimable" demands and questions, and the more of them we ask the more they become pedagogical questions to be addressed within a disciplinary space formed around the "spillage" of mistakenness. For this to happen, everything in the convergence upon the mistaken individual that marks that convergence as mimetically driven must be eliminated; and the individual himself must refrain from deflecting that convergence by instigating a convergence upon someone else. "Who are you taking me to be" is the question raised by the mistaken individual; "who are we that we take you to be whatever it is we take you to be" is the one raised by those creating a shared attention to the space. Some name in the form of the declarative sentence provides the answer to these questions.

These questions are less to be asked explicitly than to be embodied in a practice: if you're converged upon, you expose the mimetic marking in the convergence by mimicking them and responding as if you are that one; if you are among the convergent group, you name its object or target as someone to whom something has happened as well as someone who has done something, and the others in the group as those doing something and not merely addressing something that has happened. In both cases, mimetic excess is subtracted from the scene and replaced by a demythification: rather than building an identity around the stigmatized, the precise causality producing the noted result is separated more and more completely from all the other functionalities and responsibilities implicit in the situation. There are always procedures and precedents in play to facilitate this process, but proceduralism is not only insufficient, but can't even work on its own terms without placed individuals who can read the relevant procedures as imperatives bringing with them a margin of decision. The only way to be such an individual is to be prepared to present yourself as such an individual, as demonstrated in a case you are also ready to present. And the only way to ensure such individuals is through a mimological setting in which the gestures of each can be dismantled and turned into samples of practices all can inspect. There is a pedagogy of the ostensive (look not at that, but at this; not that way, but in this light); a pedagogy of the imperative (attribute everything in your act that leads to shared ostensives as following from your full faithfulness to the imperative, and the chain of imperatives it follows; attribute everything that goes awry to your failure to penetrate further layers of the imperative); and a pedagogy of the declarative (bringing all the doings and happenings within the scope of a present to the extent needed to exclude from the scene elements interfering with its minimality). The more you bring into focus some local center, the more you elucidate the terms provided by the global center making that focus possible.

Every demand is to be converted into a shared command that you are all studying together but which each of you is willing to begin obeying, and in obeying modeling a form of obedience, so as to open a space for others to retroject a form of obedience further up the chain, or follow with a subordinate and subsequent obedience—all in the name of providing objects, of representing all the participants themselves as objects, of that shared study. The central authority presumed to be at the highest point in the chain of command might be imagined to be fully secure and coherent, or in total disarray, or anywhere in between—these assessments will enter into the narratives told of the specific event, and in participating in that event you are already "foreshadowing" the contours of those possible narratives. Somewhere in there or up there must be some central authority, however embattled or potential, and you assume this central authority will be enabled by the forms of centered ordinality constitutive of coherent power. Constructing those forms of centered ordinality at any rate implies a default to some proximal power center, whose imperatives you treat as wholly consistent in themselves and with whatever central authority the proximal source of power defers to—prioritizing and temporalizing those imperatives so as to ensure their consistency is what a de-secularizing pedagogy consists of. What is needed for a restoration of the unanimity in practice towards the originating center in any social order is not (declarative) doctrines or articles of faith, but the insistence that all imperatives come from that originating center, and that everyone's contribution to filling the gap between imperatives given and imperatives obeyed can reveal that to be the case. The necessary faith for social order is that all named objects give off imperatives that we share and supplement by following imperatives up the line closer to the center. The role of declaratives is to provide order to the various imperatives: a sentence, a discourse lets us know that one is to be obeyed now, another later, another would be canceled if we properly obey the previous ones, another is to look at something rather than change it, and so on: if the imperatives are articulated in this way, the declarative tells you what to expect to see.

XXII

MAINTAINING THE PRESENT
OF THE CENTER

Once a human occupies the center, the most difficult political, and maybe human, problem, is how to replace that occupant when the time comes, as it must. We could assess different governmental forms as different ways of solving this problem, but none of them—not hereditary kingship, not democratic election—does so completely. Somewhere along the line a king will die without offspring; somewhere along the line some real or perceived failure in the electoral process will produce a president or prime minister widely considered illegitimate. I will head towards the conclusion of this book by offering a solution consistent with the originary grammar of the center I have articulated here, and along the way I will use this intrinsically anomalous element in any political order to make the various vocabularies I've been working through more inter-referential, answer some questions that might have arisen for some readers along the way, and even suggest the elements of what the Marxists call a "transitional program."

The solution I propose: the current occupant of the center chooses his successor.[1] This is, in fact, a foregone conclusion, insofar as we take power to be coherent, and all of the positions and practices in the social order to be formalized, or named. If some other body, however wide or narrow, chooses the successor, they could presumably choose the time of succession, which is to say, that body could remove the ruler at any time. In that case,

[1] For more on the approach to continuity in ruling I develop here, see my "Power and Paradox," in *Anthropoetics* XXIII, No.2, Spring 2018.

that body is the sovereign, which means that power is not organized coherently. The selection of a successor could be made on any grounds the current occupant wants, and I will stipulate here that the choice of a successor could be made for very bad reasons, leading to disastrous results. That's true of any system—democracies are obviously no more immune to the elevation of leaders destructive to the very system itself—and you wouldn't believe me if I claimed I was offering a fool-proof system. What I can do is suggest some of the considerations that would lead at least the best rulers to put in place extended institutional processes for generating candidates for selection, and that, having been institutionalized and entrenched, would likely be accepted by lesser rulers. We can simply begin with the assumption of a ruler who wants to be succeeded by the most capable person available, and the one most willing to continue the projects the current ruler considers most essential to the long-term well-being of the order he presides over.

Such a ruler would want some way of narrowing down the vast number of candidates the society in question would generate—any society will have lots of intelligent, capable, courageous young people concerned about the good of their country. The number must be narrowed down considerably—maybe to a dozen, or so. The most obvious way of doing this is by establishing special academies to produce high level government officials, and having the top 1% or so of graduates enter more grueling training and competitions to further narrow the number down. The ruler would take an intense interest in these academies, ensuring that they inculcate the most important political skills and traditions. Lower level schools would have special programs training especially qualified students to apply to those academies—the academies, then, would set the tone regarding moral, ethical and political education across the system. It may very well be that there are families and communities that have no wish to enter the system-wide competition—perhaps out of some moral or religious conviction, or because certain minorities will be disqualified from the highest offices, or they simply wish to prepare their students to participate in and express loyalty to the social order in other ways; indeed, this may very well constitute the majority.

If the educational system is heavily biased toward creating the conditions for strong candidates for succession, then that means all the disciplines will be oriented toward studying those conditions and strengthening them. Psychology, philosophy, sociology, history, economics, law, and so on, or, as I would prefer to think, the various regions of anthropomorphic pedagogy, would be primarily interested in questions of leadership and hierarchy—various forms, various causalities, better and worse forms (under different conditions), means of producing better leaders and hierarchies, means of sustaining them, and so on. After all, these are the kinds of things the candidates would need to know, and so would all those interested in the process of production and selection of candidates—and that would include at least most of the social order, insofar as local communities would be competing for and take honor from producing the best candidates most regularly. Since the process of producing candidates would be ongoing, it would be a central concern of the entire society, including, probably, the primary source of entertainment. Public competitions and ceremonies would be part of the process, as would the selection of marriage partners and family formation of the most promising candidates. Signs of the ruler's preference for one or another candidate, or one or another attribute to be privileged in the selection process, would be watched and interpreted with great interest. It would have to be the case that the ruler always has an officially designated successor, but it would also be the case that he could change this designation at any time. A long reigning ruler might no longer think the 50-year old he chose as successor 20 years ago is still right for the job; or, a candidate chosen on the assumption that rapid technological development was going to be the agenda for the next several decades might be replaced if it suddenly appears that war with a rival is likely, and a more military-oriented leader seems necessary.

All this might seem likely to create all kinds of rivalries between different candidates, and therefore resentments, the establishment of factions, bureaucratic intrigue, and so on, leading to constant instability. The way to prevent this is to prohibit the top-tier candidates from occupying positions in which they exercise any real power, which also means they are to be excluded from positions in which they make consequential decisions. Second-tier candidates and below would be elevated to higher positions of power, placed in charge of the military, industry and other high power ministries; if top tier candidates would rather have such a career, they could be given the right to renounce any aspirations to occupy the center, and be placed on a career path better suited to their ambitions. The top-tier candidates would accept the likelihood of a stunted career far below what they might have achieved otherwise, for the sake of helping maintain the coherence and continuity of the ruling order. They would be familiarized with the mechanisms of rule and, we can assume, would "intern" with the ruler—otherwise, their role would be more ceremonial, such as presiding over events, touring the country, meeting people from all walks of life. If any candidate were found to be using his role to "drum up support" or try and create a power base for himself, he would immediately be removed from consideration. Since this prohibition would be universally known, word of any attempt would get out quickly, leading to an investigation; even more, candidates would be expected to cultivate a persona that exuded, probably in an exaggerated form, disdain for flattery or offers of favors. In this way, such attitudes would also be available for emulation across the social order, raising the moral level of the people.

The selection of a successor would be the most important decision the ruler could make, and, for reasons I suggested above, it would be woven into the texture of all his other decisions: every major problem or turning point would lead to a reconsideration of the chosen successor and the arrangement of the major candidates. The ruler might want to bring them in for regular interviews to get a better sense of their fitness. Designating a new successor would be a cultural and political event, both to the ruler's subjects and other governments. Everything that a ruler should be, all the threads connecting the ruler to all other institutions, the shaping of those institutions to ensure they produce the best ruler and enable that ruler to rule—all this would be the basic substance of the culture. If this sounds strange and "cult of personality"-like, I would suggest seeing it as a social order in which the most fundamental questions of any social order—its stability, coherence and continuity—are systematically placed front and center. No one could think or speak for long without coming across questions regarding what makes this society what it is, how it could be improved, how could we do our jobs, raise our families, cultivate our intellects, develop our friendships, participate in our communities, and so on, in such a way as to contribute to that. To go back to the problem raised above, regarding the dangers of leaving so much power in one man's hands, I would say that, with the model I'm presenting here, we could say that such deeply rooted habits in the people would be very hard to repudiate, and a weak leader is more likely to rely upon them (or to have his weaknesses recuperated by them). (I also think this is a system less likely to produce weak leaders, but weakness can come in many forms and anyone could make a mistake.) In the event, the possibility of which could not be completely excluded, that a genuinely dangerous leader needed to be removed (preferably quietly, in such a way to solicit his perhaps grudging consent, with as much consensus among the elite leadership as possible), this system would provide a set of buffers lessening the shock to the system.

Now, if you are with me so far, you will acknowledge that we would be waiting for a time when the highest authority of the country we reside in will actually name his own successor. (Assuming, of course, we live, like the vast majority of the planet, in a social order not governed by a monarch.) At that point we will know that something has happened; but up until that point, what is happening is that we are waiting for that to happen. We could think of this as a kind of inverted messianism. Inverted, because everything that is shrouded in mystery in messianic expectation is made a site of pedagogy here. What would it take for whoever is formally in power right now to name his successor? What are the institutional blockages making that impossible? In our own speech and actions, we evince a readiness to commence constructing the institutional architecture (described above) in case those blockages are removed; at the same time, we act in accord with the implicit command coming from he who would have to name his successor that those blockages be respected. Whenever we deal with these institutional restraints, we represent as best we can the contrary imperatives intersecting therein, while trying to ensure the commands we transmit to others are as consistent as possible with those transmitted to us, and act so as to intimate at least the possibility of such consistency up and down the line.

This takes away from us the right, or at least the pleasure, of opposing those in power, including those we see to be most inimical to any possibility of establishing coherent forms of power. But this also doesn't mean we are obliged to become cheerleaders for whoever happens to be the president. In an insecure, incoherent system, the imperatives issuing from the center are wildly inconsistent with each other—simple, strict obedience is impossible. A hierarchy of imperatives must be constructed: there are those explicitly issued recently; older, more established ones; those inherited from previous rulers, even previous regimes, neither explicitly confirmed nor superseded; those presumed to have lapsed but capable of reactivation; and so on. The most immediate imperatives, when they cannot be complied with perfectly, must be refined in terms of more mediated ones. If you can't provide ostensive proof of compliance with the most direct imperatives, you probably won't be in a position to receive them much longer, but what will count as compliance will be determined after the fact and it's possible to comply in ways that will affect that judgment. What can always be done, though, is requesting further instructions and clarifications, and such requests can invoke the originary events of the institution and the social order. This is an instigation to archival work and the construction of alternate histories, with a search for more reliable forms of governance that were perhaps discarded or allowed to lapse but might be re-invented. There is always a mode of deferral that makes a particular imperatival space possible, and questions refer to that mode of deferral. Anyone's questions regarding the imperative chain involve an offer to donate oneself unconditionally to the center, and this donation depends upon a clarification of the centered ordinality rendering the imperative consistent. In this way, one's actions make the present anomalies transparent while seeking to resolve them. Even the most difficult cases can only be dealt with on these terms—let's say you are ordered to commit immoral acts, like atrocities, or to turn yourself over to a rigged process despite your innocence. The more your attempts at mitigation or deferral can be presented as obedience within a more expanded present, rather than the rebellion of your internal space of representation against tyranny, the more likely even your short-term prospects will improve.

Before we leave off the question of succession, it's worth noting that contemporary liberal democracy, and the US far more than any other country, has been explicitly foregrounding this question of late on its own terms. In the end, liberal democracy, whatever the textbooks say it entails ("robust media criticism of government," "independent judiciary," etc.), really comes down to peaceful transfer of power following an election. But, as we are seeing, this is an extremely complicated matter. What ensures the legitimacy of an election result? Well, obviously if the votes were miscounted, whether due to incompetence or corruption, the election is illegitimate. But who determines that, other than those who are in some way in office due to their dependence on those who have been selected by that very process? At lot of faith must be conferred here. Anyway, we're just getting started. We have further learned that the results of elections might be illegitimate if the election district has been drawn ("gerrymandered") in such a way as to favor one party over another. This is especially the case if the district has been drawn in such a way so that plausible (to whom?) claims can be made that a protected minority group has been disadvantaged. The legitimacy of elections can be diminished if the rules for determining the eligible electorate (or, for that matter, candidate) discriminate against such a group, or favor one party over another: should felons be deprived of the vote? Or for that matter, how about the placement of voting booths, or the lines upon which voters must wait in one as opposed to another venue? Why can 18 year olds vote, but not especially mature 17 year olds? What about a corrupt media that deliberately misinforms people with no other access to information? How about foreigners, who are surely impacted by the decisions made by elected officials? Once we embark on that line of thinking, why not, for an extremely influential country such as the US, enfranchise the entire world? (At this point, have we all been chastened enough by various unbelievable proposals come true to refrain from laughing?) All these questions become more contentious the more each and every element of the electoral process can be deemed to favor one side over another—and this process of politicizing presumably neutral determinations of who should be counted as a citizen and what counts as a fair process obviously feeds on itself. Now, of course, all this means nothing until one side in an election simply refuses to accept the result of that election, and mobilizes its institutional resources to contest it—we could say that the constant delegitimizing of election results in the US over the last few years (maybe decades) is a way of softening people up for this eventuality. One plausible account of the origins of elections is the concession of one side in an imminent war to another upon seeing the numbers on the other side—eventually, it becomes customary and convenient to count heads without all the trouble of actually preparing for war. Once one side refuses to accept the result of an election, we will have reverted back to the testing of all societal resources on both (all?) sides.

So, we can say, first, on a practical level, that when the existing social order starts "problematizing" succession itself, such problematization can then take on a variety of forms. And this is the case, because, second, what is put into play under such conditions is the very existence of the "people" in the name of whom representative government governs. What counts as the "people," in an operationalizable sense, is arbitrary, which is to say, depends upon histories of all kinds of power relations that cannot themselves be attributed to any decision of the people, as such decisions can only be made in previously formalized ways. A conversation over who decides what counts as "the people" is bound to be a productive one, because it makes explicit the paradoxes regarding the various ways the people supposedly chooses itself. We can parcel out all the different formal and informal elements of "the people" to different institutions, different disciplines, different starting points, and trace its construction. We will no doubt find very specific people, acting in very specific forms of concert, involved in each and every construct of the people. The people is a bit of a Frankenstein's monster, or a robot, or an android, or an army of zombies (why not draw upon the full array of popular genres for our stock of metaphors?), and it has its origin story like all of those creatures. The ongoing process of calling into question more and more of the formalized features of the electoral process, invariably in the name of some super-sovereign (a truer democracy based on a more rightly constructed "people") can be transformed into a process of modeling a process of formalization that would make questions of succession, selection and delegation everyday topics of political discourse. After all, the most likely crisis point of liberal democracy is such an outright refusal on the part of the loser in an election to accept the results, in which case these issues of political responsibility (who can secure power) would displace all the evocations of the various contending super-sovereigns.

If our focus is on the consistency and coherence of power relations, what we see in any commander-in-chief is a certain degree of interest and competence in maintaining the same. Those showing a lack of interest and competence or, even more, showing determination to further undermine the coherence of power, are the kinds of commanders we would be inclined to "oppose." Well, you could oppose them—vote against them, organize support for their opponent, write articles criticizing them, and so on. The question is whether you want a different commander-in-chief who will play the leaky power system in a way that provides you with a modicum of real or imagined power; or, whether you want to plug the leaks. If the latter, you want to develop practices, relations and institutions that would present themselves to the kinds of leaders who might name their successors as plausible replacements for the kind of officer class that thrives on leakiness. This involves minimizing reactiveness and seizing opportunities to display deferral—self-defense and tit-for-tat responses should always be framed as instituting a more coherent chain of command from the center. All the secular demands—calls for more freedom, more democracy, rights, equality, etc.—are intrinsically disordering and it will always be possible to show how more granularly constructed pedagogical relations, aimed at modeling a form of centered ordinality, would repair the situation. The truth of resentment, insofar as there is truth in it, is that power used without responsibility, or responsibility conferred without the power needed to fulfill it generates insecurity, a leaking of meaning, and therefore resentment—any analysis of conflict, then, looks for a way in which power might be matched more perfectly with responsibility.

It is also the case that the political commitment to increasing systemic incoherence will overlap significantly with "issues" as they are represented within the liberal order. Most obviously, such exploitation will almost invariably coincide with the subversion of the government's responsibility to minimize criminal activity against powerless civilians. Policies that encourage criminal activity, or raise the threshold of what is to count as criminal activity, are the calling cards of those who thrive on instability. At the same time, multiplying bureaucratically defined crimes, to be prosecuted at the discretion of officials at various levels of the system, likewise coincides with the kind of parasitism upon disorder I am discussing. We will also find that these indicators of a more uncertain political and legal setting overlap significantly with a whole range of other issues considered "cultural" and "economic"—a careful examination of policies favored across the spectrum of liberalism would yield interesting results if undertaken from the standpoint of how much tolerance and promotion of illegal and anti-social activity they would require if implemented. (If one asks, "what counts as 'genuine' as opposed to politically manufactured criminality?," one could answer as follows: genuine criminality involves acts that within an honor system the family or protector of the victim would be compelled to avenge; which is another way of saying that the purpose of a justice system is to place a ceiling on retribution permitted to those responsible for the victims.) Meanwhile, most insidious corporate activity can be eliminated in two simple ways (simple, at least if we assume a coherent regime): first, abolish anti-discrimination laws, which is what, through a predictable, even inexorable, process has led most major corporations to adopt the cultural left's agenda unconditionally; and, second, combine few, clear safety rules with a robust legal regime that can identify cause and effect and responsibility when it comes to harmful impact alleged to corporate activity—this is something we already know how to do quite well. At any rate, I am not suggesting that the current lines of political antagonism are completely unconnected with the pedagogical "expectancy" my discussion envisages.

None of this changes the fact that the goal of an onomastic pedagogy is not to address the issues but to produce the dispositions required for when some occupant of the center decides that only by passing power to a successor can the attempts he has undertaken to provide coherence to the system be sustained and continued. Naming always places the named object under the authority of the broader system of signs, or cultural authority—to name an object is to place its disposition at the disposal of the central authority. But naming is itself only effective under properly lent authority—I can call the president a traitor, or illegitimate, but those are really nothing more than desperate "suggestions" I hope some replacement will adopt—but through what chain of mediations, exactly? Better to name what the system authorizes me to name: what I am expected to do, but find it difficult to do according to expectations. I will be excluded from access to certain institutions and practices if I say something "racist," and I could protest this on "free speech" grounds, but more pertinent is the absence of anything like an acceptable definition of what counts as "racist" speech (or "sexist," "homophobic," "transphobic," and so on). Here is where a real marker of political reliability will be one's ability to resist the temptation to turn these accusations back on one's accusers, which continues the transformation of politics into attempts to be licensed as an arbiter of unacceptable speech (and into a rather pathetic simulation of the honor sysem). It will really be essential to find and create spaces where it will be possible to ask, patiently, for explanations of what, exactly, these heresies involve—how do we identify them? Who has authority to rule on violations? What does the history of precedents look like here—how would it be possible to know in advance what would count as a violation? To be blunt, it is to be demonstrated that, as I mentioned earlier, all these words mean no more and no less than the term, central to the pseudo-legal systems of all revolutionary social orders, of "counter-revolutionary." It would be impossible to overstate how transformative a patient, civil, stoic and yet uncompromising demonstration of the meaninglessness of all these words would be. You could say that without replacing those in power with different leaders, none of this would matter, as power would simply find replacements for all of them. But dissolving these words in the acid bath of their incoherence would itself do a great deal to release other power centers from externally and self-imposed limitations. To put it in originary grammatical terms: evaporating all the terms superstructured on anti-discrimination law would upset the entire ostensive order, leaving us, literally, with little to point at in a shared manner—and these are fruitful conditions for an onomastic pedagogy naming the transitions from a society of usurpers to an order saturated by pedagogical demonstrations of how to be and how to do in such a way that your practices and your life are pedagogical demonstrations.

XXIII

THE CENTER,
SPEAKING

It should be clear that I'm not calling for the restoration of the sacred—not only is it impossible to recreate ritual spaces that were predicated upon paying tribute, but it is very likely that even the most comprehensive ritualistic orders were unable to prevent the emergence of practices outside of and unrepresentable within, that order. (For that matter did any empire ever solve the problem of its "outside," Deleuze's "deterritorializers"—nomadic bands, raiders, pirates, and the rest?) To build more robust orders that will be able to name figures and practices on the outside (which any order will generate) and bring them in relation to the center, we will need increasingly rich direct representation of our sociality. The sacred is an indirect, unaware representation of sociality, since the human contribution to the construction of sacrality cannot be explicitly represented. Directly representing the social was also the project of secular thought, but the project turned out to be impossible on those terms because the "human" individual must be taken as its own origin, with the signs that mediate between humans mere expressions of what is always already internal to the human individual. The emergence of government enables a more direct representation of sociality, but as long as government is sacralized, the human contribution to sociality cannot be represented. The modern subjection of government to points of reference taken to be immediately "human" (rights, equality, nature, and so on), meanwhile, has the effect of making anti-sociality a condition of intelligibility. That is, individuals and groups can only be represented in opposition to the social, which stands in for "tyranny" or some other form of coercion (like determinism). Only by starting with a center which is both internal and external to the human, that is, a product of human practice but in its effects irreducible to any human practice, can we begin to represent sociality in more legible terms. Think of how every word or sentence we speak or write, every gesture we make, is dependent upon the millions of times those words, sentences and gestures have been deployed in extremely similar ways—by contrast, whatever is novel in any of our utterances is minimal. Part of the paradox constituting the human is that such minuscule "revisions" of the common stock of linguistic resources might have effects far beyond what the proportion between "new" and "old" in the utterance might suggest. Directly representing our sociality is paradoxical, then, because any such representation now becomes the property of our language, requiring new representations. Representations of sociality, then, are re-presentations of existing, less legible forms of sociality: they represent those forms of sociality as more differentiated, more reciprocally embedded, more centered, so that those differentiations in practices and relationships, and those elicitations of previously unacknowledged reciprocities, can become explicitly formalized designations which distribute authority and responsibilities more transparently and publicly. What I am saying here can be said in more familiar sociological, e.g., Durkheimian terms; but the specificity of representation needs to be accounted for. The line between anti-sociality and more formalized sociality is drawn through language itself. If we try and represent human or social relations directly, unmediated by the center, we will only end up representing our resentments and claims on each other, leaving us to seek some reconciliation or balance between antithetical "elements." If we take care of language, meanwhile, we will be taking care of humans, that is, each other—language always directs our attention to a center, and through that center, the center that conditions that centering.

We are all highly mediated and technologized men and women. It's staggering to think of all the ways we operate as signs across all the different media, and the way in which all of our habits, including of thought, depend upon all the devices we are plugged into. It is clear that the political vocabulary we are used to, comprised of "values," "ideas," "opinions," "agreements and disagreements," "principles," and so on, are completely inadequate for conditions where the tweak of an algorithm will determine whether 0 or 10,000 people will be exposed to something I say. To try and stand outside of, say, social media, and denounce it for isolating and manipulating and enraging people, is simply to leverage one medium—say, writing, or TV—against another, ascendant one—it's not to position us within nature against something artificial. We have to think in terms of interlocking media strategies—for example, using highly contagious maxims on Twitter to, in part, direct attention to longer essays or a book. But it's not just a question of strategy—rather, it's a question of modes of being; that is, it's ontological. If we think of ourselves as separate individuals, waging war against some tyranny on behalf of a rebellious subjectivity we are playing into well-worn strategies directed from above. Thinking in terms of group identities, however conceived, is really the same strategy on a larger scale. Thinking of ourselves as beings of the center, representatives of the center, delegates, emissaries of the center, opens up new possibilities. In that case we're offering the central authority feedback based upon the difficulties we're having in fulfilling imperatives coming from the central authority. Among those imperatives are, certainly, ones directing us to individualize (self-center) ourselves in certain ways, and to organize ourselves into communities along certain lines. Every imperative from the center—every law, every invocation of a constitutional obligation, every priority suggested by some government action—necessarily suggests various modes of individuation and corporatization. Again, the point is not simply to drop all the ways you have of thinking about yourself, but to see those ways as always already in a kind of asymmetrical exchange with the center. What is wanted is to have those identities named, and the imperatives following upon that naming to be drawn out.

The various media and technologies, then, are our articulation with and through the center. Questions of whether technologies dehumanize us, or interfere with our privacy or personal freedoms are always questions posed, futilely, from within an older media to a newer one. Even more specifically, it may be that most of these criticisms come from an imagined experience of mid-20th century urban living, where for many a certain balance among the desires of prosperity, freedom from externally imposed norms, and sociality was possible. However that may be, the central authority will always want to know enough about the people it governs to govern them; and the governed are also filled with expectations regarding the maintenance of safety, conditions for forming families, engaging in productive activity and enjoyment that always already presuppose a central imaginary seeing to spatial arrangements and information gathering. A demand that I be left alone entails a whole series of assumptions about my relations with others. Even more, it assumes the existence of projects I am or could be engaged in with others, either directly or by proxy. Imagine stripping from our discussion all references to "rights," on the one hand, and notions of "checks and balances," or "public and private," on the other hand, and consider what discussions of the relationship between individuals, communities, corporations and governments would then look like. The only way we could get our bearings without those familiar legal and political markers is by isolating another, also familiar one: the notion of "chartering," central to Western culture, at least, since the Middle Ages, and in a way Roman antiquity. If everything is chartered—corporations, profit and non-profit, subordinate units of government—as, in fact, is already the case, then as individuals we are always already all chartered up. Questions of social order then come down to clarifying the terms of the charters issued at all levels, and the only agency capable of doing that is the sovereign, and sovereign agents. Charters bind all agencies to the imperatives of the center. To the extent that we're all agents of the sovereign, even if not to the same degree of officiality, our main contribution to public discourse is clarifying the operations of the institutions we participate in in terms of their charters and our own competencies. To the extent of our abilities, we clarify and represent the kind of scenes the media we participate in place us upon: at the very least, this means incorporating, in the way each medium allows, the feedback of actual and possible audiences, and reconstructing one's centeredness accordingly; and, it means that it is as "pieces" within the "technosphere" that we create fractal pedagogical hierarchies. These practices are part of listening to the center.

What will happen once one ruler selects his successor is that we will see relations reduced to sovereign-to-sovereign ones, without the mediation of a whole conglomerate of shifting and unaccountable agencies. The reduction of all relationships to such formalized ones: ruler to ruler, ruler to delegate, delegate to delegate, ultimately including everyone in an ordered way—that is the way out of liberalism, on the international as well as national level. As terrifying as it may sound to some, such an order in fact expects the most of its people, wherever they are situated within hierarchies. What is absolutely forbidden under such an order is directing violent centralization toward the authorities—and that target is the source of all violent centralizations, which always, at whatever scale, seek to find and punish a hidden power imagined to lie behind the scenes of the official power. Authorities are never opposed as authorities—no one is ever, in practice, an anarchist—but as usurped authorities, at which point we enter the realm of the super-sovereigns we invoke to do battle against usurping tyrants. If we can't charge the authorities with usurpation, our resentments must be constructed according to the terms of redress and remediation constructed by those authorities themselves. If those terms of redress and remediation turn out to be applied in an "unjust," even "absolutely" unjust way, on their own terms, it will be recognized that directing resentment toward those institutions or those who staff them cannot possibly correct those injustices. To assume that it can is to assume that the temporality of resentment is commensurate with the temporality of institutional rectification. With all the means available, one provides feedback to the system, but it is a mark of advanced deferral to acknowledge that the effective recipient of that feedback cannot be anticipated within the feedback itself. Even if we consider the necessity of disobeying an unambiguously immoral order, such an act must be presented as a sign of what will eventually come to be regarded as obedience—not to some higher power, but to that very, for the moment shortsighted, power. Leaving testimony for agents of the regime to examine is a repudiation of any instigation of a revolt against the system. This renunciation of the temptation to occupy an internal scene of representation in rebellion against the tyrant in the name of some super-sovereign is what we can call "donating your resentment to the center."

Media and technology are, as Marshall McLuhan noted, extensions of our senses and body. McLuhan seems to be imagining a "natural" body made "artificial," though, which paradoxically presupposes some kind of control center "using" those extensions, as if they were deliberately developed as prosthetics. The situation looks different once we consider technology, media and capital as means of generating asymmetrical reciprocity between center and margins. The elements of the originary scene is itself the first media, and we use it to "keep an eye" on each other, while turning ourselves into "limbs" ready to restrain anyone interfering with the visual apparatus, and into measuring rods dividing up portions. Now that eyes are literally everywhere, each of us can transform surveillance and recording devices into our eyes and ears; now that calculating probabilities of human action has been automated, we can all transform machinic algorithms into our brains; we each have our own access to wheels and wings; and so on. Now, instead of plugging these observations into an oceanic feeling of global communality, consider what is involved in coordinating all the "organs" of these bodies, that each of us participates in from our respective positions on the margin. So, when I see something (say, a video making the rounds of Twitter), it means something to the extent that one of the "legs" (or wings or wheels) I have anthropomorphized out of the technological nerves, bones and muscles I operate within gets me close enough to what I see so that my "hands" (e.g., security guards able to stop an appalling situation) can "touch" and "handle" things; or, perhaps, that one of the voices I've anthropomorphized as an echo or amplification or translation of my own can command those "hands" to operate in that way. If I want to increase the efficacy of these "motor functions" so that what I see and hear can be more closely integrated into what I say, which in turn contributes to my transformation of things happening to me into things I do then I need to think about where such coordination is already taking place, because then I can know where to move within the system. Where seeing, hearing, doing, happening, saying, thinking and knowing are all moving in the same way, that's where the center needs to be, and to some extent already is. The center is the coordination I'm seeking within the circuits of capital, technology and media, and every attempt to contribute to greater coordination is in obedience to the imperative of the center. I may be wrong at any time, but if I'm wrong, it's about the transmission and full implications of an imperative that tells me to defer some resentment at having been compelled to coordinate, and others can correct and improve my effort. I may imagine I can see and "grasp" everything I need to, but my vision and reach is in fact partial relative to projections of my power; it's not that the occupant of the center is all seeing, knowing, doing, and so on (he does all that through us)—rather, it is only in attempting to enhance the commands coming from the center by animating whatever organs within organs respond to my motions that it can even make sense to think of increasing my own motor functioning.

The most powerful and contributory form of agency within what Benjamin Bratton calls "The Stack" is that of the designer. The origins of the modern individual with an inviolate internal scene of representation lie in what Gans calls the Christian revelation, which forbids targeting the individual for sacrifice in order to save the community. Sacrifice is interdicted because the Christian revelation revealed sacrifice to be a temporary resolution to a permanent mimetic crisis, and one which conceals those mimetic roots by constructing myths of the victim and the event of sacrifice. If the individual is to be immune to sacrificial inclinations, culture must be reorganized so as to study and pre-empt those inclinations, at an increasingly early stage. This entails constructing profiles of both individuals and the community, since features of the individual would elicit scapegoating tendencies by giving off signs that evoke memories of previous crises. It would be necessary to recode behavioral triggers so as to inhibit both anomalous behaviors and pre-inscribed responses to such behaviors. In the process—as a way of facilitating the process—it is possible to attribute to individuals all kinds of characteristics, faculties and essences. The individual has a soul, has free will, has a moral law inscribed within, has consciousness, and so on. All this is a mythicization of the individual: all we really need to do is assume that, with the interdiction of violent centralization, each individual (each language user) is obliged and provided a space to self-construct as a center in relation to other centers and the Center. Rather than an internal scene of representation, then, we have narrated practices of centering, which vary widely across circumstances and as the relations between center and margin change. What happens as the interdiction is installed is the construction of modes of "normalization" studied by Michel Foucault and other thinkers, who have traced them back to early Christian practices of asceticism and confession, and which come to fix the relation between the individual and the central authority. It's not surprising that such systems of normalization have been autonomized via the algorithmic imperative of the contemporary social-technological order. The autonomization of normalization provides socialized material for individuals to work on in constructing self-centering representations, representations that can be as wide in scope as the individual's power extends. The exercise of this power is design—the design of practices that reframe resentments as means of donation to the center. We can all, at least, design our immediate practices; to varying degrees, we can also suggest institutional designs and educate each other in their production.

Marcel Jousse, in his book on the "Galilean" oral tradition, *Memory, Memorization and Memorizers: The Galilean Oral-Style Tradition and its Traditionists*, which has Jesus ("Yeshua") at the center, points to the cultural productivity of what he calls the "transfer translation." The transfer translation was a translation of sacred texts, written in a now lesser known language, into the language currently spoken by the people. Since these sacred texts were rich in features of language that went well beyond what we normally think of as "content," such as metaphors built into the language, rhyme, rhythm, associations, allusions, and so on, the problem for the transfer translation was to carry all of this over into the new language. It was never completely successful:

> Unfortunately, in its brevity, the transfer-targum did not always, simultaneously, embrace clear simplicity. It could not, for a variety of psychological, historical, and ethnic reasons. A targum would always, arguably and variably, confirm the maxim: *traduttore, traditore*. Therefore, in the case of the transfer-targum, it was a pedagogical necessity to carry alongside it, or better still, within it, its elucidating "explanation," its "midrash." From the time of the first targumization of Esdras, the entire rhythmo-catechistics of the Palestinian Rabbis were no more than a huge midrash-explication of the traditional formulae of the Hebraic Torah in scholastic Hebrew, or its Aramaic transfer-targum in popular Aramaic. (336)

The "midrash," and this would also apply to myths, legends, proverbs, folktales, wisdom literature, and so on, are products of attempts to redeem the transfer translation: to ensure, and confirm, that the text is the same. What Jousse describes here is consistent with my early discussion of the generation of myth out of the failures of imperative exchange between margin and center; it is also an attempt to maintain linguistic presence. Our own discourses are no less attempts to determine that the signs we are using and practices we are participating in remain the same as we continually translate them (even the same words, which keep changing in meaning and use) from one form into another—our narratives are work on reconciling "mistranslations." The individual who enters the normalizing space as a designer trains his attention directly on the relation between "source" and "target" languages, which can itself be accessed through anomalies in the "(mis)translations." There is always a mismatch between what we demand of the world and what we take the world to be demanding of us—we try to translate one into the other so as to make them commensurable. This is the logic of imperative exchange, or sacrifice, which can never be abolished once and for all, but can continually be translated into donations to the center. An "instinctive" response to a provocation (or "usurpation") can be withheld so that time is given to imagine a form of interaction that would redirect the reactive cycle itself—this would involve designing scenes of centered ordinality that would have suspended (and can still "have suspended") the usurpation by proposing a pedagogically embedded space for each and all. Producing mappings, architecture, institutional devices, the creation of events ("happenings"), the projection of future possibilities would be among the forms taken by the compositions of "selves" ("self" really just means "the same," that is, the same as one was the last time referred to). Political practice would ideally involve exposing the Rube Goldberg-like designs of liberalism while simultaneously proposing and embodying designs articulating new layers of deferral.

The mistaken space opened by the transfer translation is the source of narratives as objects, centers that we were attending from but now attend to, issues imperatives that we trace back to the center by designing scenes upon which we all see the same object, in the same aspect. The most elemental transfer translation is of the same word, from one text and form of embeddedness to another. (An obvious example would be a word like "racist"—in ensuring that "racist" from a text published in 1967 is the same as "racist" in a new broadcast in 2020, what kind of stories would we have to tell?) You design the world so that objects narrate possibilities within which you name yourself as a character obeying the center by drawing from objects and events, and in the face of abundantly displayed counter-evidence, signs that its occupant might select its own successor. Whatever idioms—religious, political, philosophical, aesthetic—you presently inhabit can be redesigned so as to supply the names needed for such narratives. And if they can't be so redesigned, what good are they? But they probably can be, albeit more through enactment than cogitation. Where an ostensive is, there an imperative will be; and where an imperative, an interrogative and corresponding declaratives. All through a series of mistakes, of course—mistakes that can't themselves be designed but which can be designed for. The line between what all of us on a scene, in a disciplinary space, see as the same thing, and that point at which differences start creeping in, can be identified and therefore controlled for, even if the conversion of a difference into an imperative can't be predicted (and, in fact, its unpredictability should also be designed for through a wide field of possible differences). A broad range of mistake driven moral and aesthetic innovations thereby work their way through the filtering mechanism to the center.

Now, I want to conclude this way so that I make it clear that, how, and why anthropomorphics eliminates humanism; but also to show that originary grammar identifies the always already becoming human that makes it impossible to think of any post- or transhuman project as anything other than a series of distributed attempts to declaratively hierarchize commands from the center so that in re-centering those attempts we pose the kinds of questions that open new ostensive regions. And we can learn to see any utterance in terms of if and how it opens up those ostensive regions. In the end, a human science needs no more "proof" of anything other than what people say (in relation to what other people say, have said, might say…). All we can say (through whatever media) is what the center has us say, and that the center has us say it. You talk about something, and in doing so make a place for that thing; that place, then, as a center, is assailed by some, and inhabited by other, interested parties; you invoke some other center to convert the convergence into a sign of the endurance of the thing in its place; your utterances are in turn marked by more or less implicit references to that other center; those markings in your discourse make you a center as they are noted by others; if you can become a center for others you can inhabit the place where you become so and your discourse can become a center for yourself; everything you say, then, counts as saying insofar as it is marked by a reliance on the center becoming invisible by marking the visible, and it is so marked insofar as it makes that center even less visible because it is a sheer effect of its visible representatives all maintaining the places enabling you to say what you are saying and that you are saying it. We become more human, that is, more capable of deferral and constructions of inviolate reality, insofar as less and less is said about the center and all of our doings become the articulated representation of the center, that is at the same time the retrieval of distributed effects of ever more distant centers.

Why should you believe what anyone else says? Because they provide "proof"? Have they also proven the proof—that is, provided the criteria for determining what counts as proof, and that those criteria have been met in this case? Or, for that matter, why those criteria? Or that what was meant to be proven was relevant or meaningful in the first place? But we have to beware of hucksters, shills and grifters, and so there must be some way of distinguishing the manipulative and self-serving from the true, the good, the reliable and the sustainable. Note that the problem here is the discrepancy between what is said and what is meant (that is, what maintains the consistency of what is said over time). This is a problem opened up by the destruction of sacred order, in which utterances match their context and meaning insofar as they are authorized by the ritual center. The problem can therefore only be solved by abolishing secular disorder in a formalized sociality and centered ordinality. But it must be addressed in the still ongoing and likely to be prolonged interregnum represented by secularity. For starters, we can ask to see a demonstration of a readiness to play whatever role within a given order is required: that is, to be a center oneself, or preserve another's centrality. Can you shift across the grammatical persons (first, second, third; singular, plural) when dangerous attention is converging on one of them? We could speak of a commensurability of ostensive, imperative, interrogative and declarative dispositions. Do the commands, demands, and requests you issue have shared ostensive endpoints? Do the questions you ask pinpoint some ostensive confusion and help to clarify what we're talking about? Can one trace a line from your declaratives to the ostensives that would make them meaningful? Can you sustain the present tense? (lapses into the past suggest attempts to justify; leaps into the future desperate promises) But the way to answer all these questions is not to construct canons of proof that would, say, mark some deficiency in an imperative-ostensive articulation. Rather it is to model your practice on the one upon whom you might rely—to match, insert, inflect, amplify, distribute those practices and build hypothetical and real orders, uninfiltratable, and filled with redundancies, out of them. The question of whether to rely on him in the first place must have resulted from some disruption of your practices, some infiltration, the other's practices have generated, so only a new order will answer the question. The proof will be in the creation of orders that generate other orders and replace without unnecessary disturbance lesser orders. This is what "grace" means in the retrieval of centered ordinality.

The disciplines turn into ongoing language learning. Language never exists as a single object that could be comprehensively described, as it is always being changed by the latest utterance. Each of us then represents language in one of its manifestations, and so human interaction always involves learning the language of the other—taking the words and sentences (and gestures, tone, images, and so on) of others and iterating them to ensure that we have the same sign for the purpose of eliciting a particular center. We don't need a comprehensive and universally shared philosophy or faith, then—how could such a thing even be possible, given that we all know what words like "think" and "know" mean, since all languages have equivalents of these words, and any attempt to discern a "realer" form of knowing would have to use words that ultimately would have to rely on the word "know" for their meaning; and that words like "belief" don't refer to some kind of inner experience but are "markers of sincerity" reinforcing something one says (and, really, interfere with sorting out the imperatives coming to use from the revelatory event that has riveted our attention)? Now, in learning the language of the other, you necessarily use their words in mistaken ways, as that is the essence of language learning. Each such mistake constitutes a break in linguistic presence, and hence a potential mimetic crisis, even if not always equally consequential. All the competing discourses out there are differing modes of language learning, which therefore means differing modes of deferring the crisis implicit in instances of mistakenness. This entails converting mistakes into idioms which generate new ostensive fields. The better discourses are those that can effect such conversions on all other discourses, turning the centrifugal resentments lurking in mistaken "transfers" of terms to new uses into proposals for new deferrals. That is, the better discourses are the ones that know they are engaged in language learning, and that language learning is the soliciting of the center. All discourses and disciplinary spaces are compatible with each other, even if none will leave their reciprocal encounters intact. Demands for truth-claims, sincerely held, and for explanations, provable or falsifiable, are all to be converted into representations of the kind of space in which such claims could be resolved ostensively and the practices required to so represent them, and this is another way of carrying words over from a declarative setting through imperative and ostensive ones. Instead of trying to prove someone is wrong, why not just carry over their words, asking what if you say this here, and here, and here? If they are indeed wrong, their words will come out of the process different, and no longer their own. If they're right and you're wrong, though, the iteration of their words across all those actual and hypothetical uses will yield more uses that will be inter-referential with the others. If this seems anarchistic or relativistic, consider that such a practice of languaging would never allow anyone to challenge the legitimacy of any government or form of authority—it removes the entire background against which legitimacy can be assessed. But it still presupposes that entire structure of authority, as none of the linguistic practices I've been describing could be conducted without it. All there would be to talk about are the various imperative gaps emerging at all points within the structure and how to extend ourselves across them. So there would be no need for aggressive questioning like, "who decides when new uses of language are 'inter-referential' or not," because such tiresome invocations of some phantom authority are no longer meaningful once we're no longer trying to get "behind" authority. One can simply be invited to make them more inter-referential, or to caricature the latest representation of inter-referentiality—and probably in the meantime other imperative gaps will have presented themselves to our attention.

BIBLIOGRAPHY

Bartlett, Andrew. *Mad Scientist, Impossible Human: An Essay in Generative Anthropology.* The Davies Group Publishers, 2014.

——————. "From First Hesitation to Scenic Imagination: Originary Thinking with Eric Gans." In *Contagion: Journal of Violence, Mimesis and Culture,*" Vol. 15-16 (2008/2009), 89-172.

——————. "Accusations of 'Playing God' and the Anthropological Idea of God," in Katz, 2007, 299-350.

——————. "Originary Science, Originary Memory, Frankenstein and the Problem of Modern   Science." *Anthropoetics* XII, No. 2, Fall 2006/Winter 2007.

Berman, Joshua. *Created Equal: How the Bible Broke with Ancient Political Thought.* Oxford University Press, 2011.

Bond, C.A. *Nemesis: The Jouvenelian vs. Liberal Model of Human Orders.* Imperium Press, 2019.

Bratton, Benjamin. *The Stack: On Software and Sovereignty.* The MIT Press, 2016.

De Jouvenel, Bertrand. *Sovereignty.* Liberty Fund, Inc., 1998.

——————. *On Power: The Natural History of its Growth.* Liberty Fund, Inc., 1993.

Derrida, Jacques. "Structure, Sign and Play in the Human Sciences." In *Writing and Difference*. Translated by Alan Bass. Univeristy of Chicago Press, 1978, 278-294.

Fustel De Coulanges, Numa Denis. *The Ancient City*. Imperium Press, 2020.

Gans, Eric. *The Origin of Language: A New Edition*. Edited with and introduction by Adam Katz. Spuyten Duyvil, 2019.

——————. *Science and Faith: The Anthropology of Revelation*. New Edition. The Davies Group Publishers, 2015.

——————. "On the One Medium." In *Mimesis, Movies and Media: Violence, Desire and the Sacred, Volume 3*, Edited by Scott Codwell, Chris Fleming and Joel Hodge, Bloomsbury Academic, 2015, 7-16.

——————. *A New Way of Thinking: Generative Anthropology in Religion, Philosophy, Art*. The Davies Group Publishers, 2011.

——————. *Signs of Paradox: Irony, Resentment, and Other Mimetic Structures*. Stanford University Press, 1997.

——————. *Originary Thinking: Elements of Generative Anthropology*. Stanford University Press,   1993.

——————. *The End of Culture: Toward a Generative Anthropology*. University of California Press, 1985.

Girard, Rene. *The Scapegoat*. Translated by Yvonne Freccero. John Hopkins University Press, 1989.

——————. *Deceit, Desire and the Novel: Self and Other in Literary Structure*. Translated by Yvonne Freccero. John Hopkins University Press, 1965.

Graeber, David. *Debt: The First 5,000 Years. Updated and Expand-*

ed. Melville House, 2014.

——————. and Marshall Sahlins. *On Kings.* HAU, 2017.

Hill, Dan. *Dark Matter and Trojan Horses: A Strategic Design Vocabulary.* Strelka Press, 2012.

Hui, Yuk. *Recursivity and Contingency.* Rowman and Littlefield Publishers, 2019.

Katz, Adam, ed. *The Originary Hypothesis: A Minimal Proposal for Humanistic Inquiry.* The Davies Group Publishers, 2007.

——————. "Book Review: Nemesis: The Jouvenelian vs. the Liberal Model of Human Orders." *Anthropoetics* XXV, No. 1, Fall 2019.

——————. "Generative Anthropology as the One Big Discipline." *Anthropoetics* XXIV, No. 2,   Spring 2019.

——————. "Power and Paradox." *Anthropoetics* XXIII, No. 2, Spring 2018.

——————. "An Introduction to Disciplinarity." *Anthropoetics* XX, No. 2, Spring 2015.

——————. "Attentionality and Originary Ethics: Upclining." *Anthropoetics* XIX, No. 1, Fall 2013.

——————. "Originary Mistakenness, Defilement and Modernity." *Anthropoetics* XVI, No. 1, Fall 2010.

Jousse, Marcel. *Memory, Memorization and Memorizers: The Galilean Oral-Style Tradition and its Traditionists.* Cascade Books, 2018.

——————. *The Oral Style.* Routledge, 2016.

——————. Edited by Edgard Sienaert. *In Search of Coherence.*

Pickwick Publications, 2016.

Latour, Bruno. *Reassembling the Social: An Introduction to Actor-Network Theory*. Oxford University Press, 2007.

MacIntyre, Alasdair. *After Virtue: A Study in Moral Theory, Third Edition*. University of Notre Dame, 20007.

Mumford, Lewis. *Technics and Civilization*. University of Chicago Press, 2010.

Oakley, Francis. *Kingship: The Politics of Enchantment*. Wiley-Blackwell, 2006.

Olson, David R. *The Mind on Paper: Reading, Consciousness and Rationality*. Cambridge University Press, 2019.

—————. *Psychological Theory and Educational Reform: How School Remakes Mind and Society.* Cambridge University Press, 2003.

—————. *The World on Paper: The Conceptual and Cognitive Implications of Reading and Writing*. Cambridge University Press, 1996.

Peirce, Charles Sanders. *Philosophical Writings of Peirce*. Edited by Justus Buchler. Dover Publications, 2011.

Polanyi, Michael. *The Tacit Dimension*. University of Chicago Press, 2009.

Rieff, Philip. *Charisma: The Gift of Grace and How It Has Been Taken from Us*. Pantheon, 2007.

Seaford, Richard. *Money and the Early Greek Mind: Homer, Philosophy, Tragedy*. Cambridge University Press, 2004.

Tomasello, Michael. *A Natural History of Human Thinking*. Harvard University Press, 2014.

——————. *Origins of Human Communication (Jean Nicod Lectures)*. A Bradford Book, 2010.

——————. *Constructing a Language: A Usage-Based Theory of Language Acquisition*. Harvard University Press, 2005.

Van Oort, Richard. "Imitation and Human Ontogeny: Michael Tomasello and the Scene of Joint Attention." In *Anthropoetics* XIII, No. 1, Spring/Summer 2007.

Wierzbicka, Anna. *Imprisoned in English: The Hazards of English as a Default Language*. Oxford   University Press, 2013.

——————. *Experience, Evidence and Sense: The Hidden Cultural Legacy of English*. Oxford University Press, 2010.

——————. *Cross-Cultural Pragmatics*. De Gruyter Mouton, 2003.

——————. *Emotions Across Languages and Cultures: Diversity and Universals*. Cambridge University Press, 1999.

——————. *The Semantics of Grammar*. John Benjamins Publishing Company, 1988.

GLOSSARY

Attentional space: This concept draws upon the work of psychologist and linguist Michael Tomasello upon the signifying capacities of apes and humans. Tomasello's finding that apes, unlike even very small children, do not point (in order to show something to another) is taken to offer confirmation of Eric Gans's "originary hypothesis," which strongly suggests that the first sign, differentiating humans from other advanced hominids, was a gesture pointing towards a central object. Tomasello uses the concept of "joint attention" to designate this specifically human capacity: again, like on the hypothetical originary scene, what is specific to humans is our capacity to attend to some thing jointly with others—and for each to be aware of the other's attention to that thing. Any situation in which humans share attention in this way is what I call an "attentional space."

Attentionality: I constructed this concept by analogy with the very familiar phenomenological concept of "intentionality," which most technically refers to the conscious apprehension of some object within a frame but is more generally used to refer to actions taken consciously and deliberately. My purpose here is to insist on "attention" as a stage prior to "intention" and, in fact, as including "intention" in itself. Thinking in terms of "attentionality" rather than "intentionality" emphasizes the constitutively social form of our thought and action, and allows us to ground the declarative order in the ostensive-imperative world.

Big Man: This is a term I borrow from Eric Gans who, in his *The*

175

End of Culture, borrows it from the anthropologist Marshall Sahlins. It is important for generative anthropology because it marks the moment at which the sacred center, which was at first occupied only by the sacred object itself (presumably the totemic and appetitive object of the group), comes to be occupied by a human. This moment marks the beginning of explicit and "legitimated" inequality between humans.

Centered ordinality: Eric Gans had seen the originary event as one in which all members of the group issued the first sign (the aborted gesture of appropriation) simultaneously. It seemed to me that this couldn't be the case, and that if the crisis leading up to the emission of the sign was mimetically driven, the same must be the case, in reverse, so to speak, for the issuing of the sign. Someone, then, must have put forth the gesture (a kind of hesitation) first, with others subsequently imitating that sign. So, if there's a first, there's also a second, and a third, and so on. This establishment of a sequential order then, it seemed to me, must be taken as the model for human activity as such, and "centered ordinality" seemed to express that directly.

Cultural form: Much of what I do in the book is take concepts created by Eric Gans as he followed through on the implications of his originary hypothesis and apply them in ways that to my mind were more thorough, consistent and insistent. So, in his first book laying out the implications of the originary hypothesis, *The Origin of Language*, Gans shows how language must have developed from the first, ostensive, sign, through the imperative, the interrogative and then the declarative sentence. In two subsequent books, *The End of Culture* and *Originary Thinking*, Gans pursued this idea by distinguishing between ostensive, imperative and declarative "cultures." But he didn't see fit to develop this into an overall theoretical vocabulary. I thought this was a very productive avenue to explore since we are clearly always "inside" of signs and therefore should be able to describe all human activities and relations in terms of these basic linguistic forms. In this I was also inspired by Charles Sanders Peirce's semiotic project, which aimed at reducing all human sign activity (which is all human activity) to some articulation of iconic, indexical and symbolic signs. There is a rough parallel between iconic/ostensive, index/imperative, symbol/declarative. Various ethical, moral and intellectual implications then followed from this inquiry. Perhaps most importantly for anthropomorphics, it seemed to me that replacing what I regarded as the mostly rote and empty discourses of subjectivity, involving "wills," "desires," "intentions," "consciousness," "conscience" and so on, all of which must be supposed to be "somewhere" "inside" us, with the notion of chains of imperatives, we could speak about the sociality and historicality of our practices in a whole new way. We often say things like "I felt compelled to…"—so, why not take that a little bit more literally and posit an imperative, rooted in tradition and social hierarchies, that is being obeyed? Since, on Gans's account in *The Origin of Language*, the declarative came into being as a kind of interruption of an "inappropriate imperative," we could say that there is a permanent tension between these two speech forms, and that this tension between the immediacy required by imperative structures and the delay and questioning introduced by declarative structures, could in turn give us new and more productive ways of talking about historical breaks and social dysfunctions.

Disciplinary space: We all know what a "discipline" is—an academic or professional space, institutionalized and subject to some rules of entry and standards of performance, that is focused on some subject matter or area. It seemed to me that at the origin of every discipline there must be the creation of a new attentional space. A new "object" comes into view, as one "paradigm" is replaced by another. I'm guided here by the theory of scientific development and discovery associated with thinkers like Thomas Kuhn, Gaston Bachelard and others—but the fact that all of the moral and intellectual transformations we associate with the "Axial Age," such as early Christianity, Greek Philosophy and Chinese philosophy also involved the creation of spaces of conversation, devoted to "higher" and more permanent questions, separated from everyday life also seemed important here. The development of new attentional spaces into disciplines is inevitable—the attentional space, strictly speaking, was never real outside of some discipline. But for the discipline to remain active, the origin of the discipline in some new form of attention needs to be recreated. This recreation, or iteration, of the origin of the discipline within the discipline, is what I've been calling "disciplinary spaces." Of course, disciplinary spaces can emerge on the margins of disciplines, or at intersections between disciplines.

Firstness: the concept of "firstness" derives from my modification of the originary event under the assumption that one of the members of the group must have issued the sign first, to be in turn imitated by the others. In any human activity, someone goes first, and it matters who goes first. I take the notion of "firstness" to be useful for breaking up lazy invocations of some "we," which presuppose spontaneous group action. "Firstness" is a way of speaking about responsibility, of "stepping into the breach." It's also, though, a way of breaking up assumptions about the unity of consciousness and intentionality because the one who goes first can't really be quite sure what he's done until others follow and complete the event. Charles Sanders Peirce's notion of an experiential "firstness" linked to iconic signs, which are grasped immediately and intuitively, was certainly in my mind in first using the concept, and the two uses of the term are related insofar as in both cases "firstness" isn't "actual" until we have a second and third.

Fractal hierarchy: Benoit Mandelbrot's concept of "fractals" is pretty familiar by now. The simplified sense in which I use it is that the micro level reiterates (or is reiterated by) the macro level. If you zero in on a very small part of a coastline, which looks smooth from a distance, you will see patterns (articulations of angles and shapes) very similar to what is seen on the coastline as a whole. I don't know about coastlines, but the notion that micro-relations that seem smooth and undifferentiated from a distance, and can therefore serve as a contrast to more obviously differentiated large scale social relations, are in fact just as differentiated and broken up as the larger institutions seems to me a very productive hypothesis. Here, I apply it to so-called "egalitarian" relationships in small groups, which are often contrasted, for utopian or anarchist purposes, with the pervasive "inequalities" of our squalid everyday life. Following the concepts of "firstness" and "centered ordinality," it becomes possible to assert that, looked at more closely, supposed egalitarian relations are just as riven by inequalities as large scale institutions. In any conversation, even an easygoing one between close friends, someone dominates or sets the agenda for the conversation; at the very least, one is talking and one is listening, at any given moment. These are "fractal hierarchies," and since they are pervasive and constitutive, we can also say they are not bad, and thereby shift our attention from devising schemes for eliminating inequalities to designing more orderly and beneficial hierarchies.

Gesture of aborted appropriation: This is one of the founding concepts of Generative Anthropology. According to Eric Gans's concept of the originary event, the gesture of aborted appropriation is the first sign, which is to say, the first use of language. With all of the members of a group moving and reaching towards some central object, the pre-human pecking order breaks down and, with appetite intensified by mimetic desire, a violent conflict threatening the survival of the group is imminent. One member, then another, aborts the move towards appropriation. This aborted move converts appropriation into a gesture signifying a renunciation of appropriation. All language, and all rituals and human institutions follow from this gesture, and are therefore something like this gesture. A more radical way of putting it is that all of human life and culture is a continuation of that gesture.

Imperative exchange: This is a concept I derived from Gans's analysis of early human culture, in its imperative and preliminary declarative stage, in *The End of Culture*. The first relation of the human group to the sacred center is ostensive, with the emergence of rituals iterating the originary event. The emergence of the imperative generates a new stage in human culture: beyond just "pointing" to the center, members of the group can issue imperatives to the center. These imperatives would not be commands, but supplications and requests—what we call "prayers." The human group is always involved in some kind of exchange with the central object: at the ostensive stage, the human group "honors" the sacred center and, in return, is granted its very existence. So, if the group is now issuing imperatives to the center, it must also be hearing imperatives from it. Like any exchange, it has the form of *do ut des*: I give so that you may give. It is simultaneously a gift exchange—gifts are what are being requested and commanded. This is the logic of sacrifice. I apply this concept more generally to the structure of all imperatives. If some individual "does what he is supposed to," that is, follows social imperatives, in exchange he expects the social order to at least protect him from certain harms. This is the structure of our mimetic relation to "reality." The concept of "imperative exchange" also provides us with a way of specifying the relation between declaratives and imperatives. On the most basic level, declaratives "explain" the failures of imperative exchanges. If I did what the sacred being at the center commanded, but my hunt nevertheless was fruitless, this must be accounted for: perhaps I did what was commanded, but not with the right "intention." Perhaps some opponent of the sacred being interfered with its intention. We can see the origin of mythology here. Similarly, a modern individual who has "played by the rules" but has nevertheless had his expectations of a good life frustrated will find narratives and analyses that invent agencies responsible for this discrepancy.

Imperative gap: In a sense, this concept is simple: there is a difference between the imperative that is issued and the one that is obeyed. No imperative can completely specify the terms of its implementation. Some discretion is necessarily left to the obedient. This is important in my originary grammar because this concept gives us a new way of thinking about what makes a command "legitimate." Instead of asking whether a command corresponds to some external concept of "justice" (so that one is within one's rights to refuse to obey an "unjust" order), one would now think within the terms set by the imperative itself. The imperative is not even taken to be legitimate a priori—it's more that the concept of "legitimacy" doesn't apply to imperatives. The question is not whether to obey, but how to obey or which to obey, and the answer is to be found in closing the imperative gap, which means making the imperative one is obeying as consistent as possible, in itself and in its dependence upon previous imperatives—those issued by the authority in question and those that founded the social order or authorized the authority. This doesn't necessarily make questions of obedience easier, but it has us starting with authority as the default condition, rather than as contingent upon some ultimately arbitrary concept.

Imperative interrogativity: Imperative exchange is a sacrificial order: I give up something, some part of myself, and in return, the gods, God or some hypostasized concept of "society" or 'reality" will give me something. Ultimately, this kind of order must reach its limits. Declaratives will only be able to go so far in "rationalizing" at least some of the more egregious discrepancies between what the individual gives and what the individual receives. Moreover, there is an escalatory logic to imperative exchange, or the gift economy, or sacrificial logic, whereby what the center has given is incommensurable with anything one could give in return. According to Rene Girard, whose account is accepted in its essentials by Eric Gans, the sacrifice of Jesus exposes the limits of sacrifice, or what I call imperative exchange. If we're thinking sacrificially, we are looking for something that we own that can be given to the center. When sacrifice fails, it makes sense to up the ante—to increase the sacrifice so as to appease whatever being we place at the center. This logic eventually leads us to human sacrifice. This is the logic exposed by Jesus's self-sacrifice—all the "reasons" given for killing Jesus are fraudulent and driven by sacrificial logics. "All" Jesus said was, in essence, stop scapegoating (sacrificing) some member of the community—this is not what God wants. For this, he was sacrificed. Acknowledging Jesus's sacrifice means that we can no longer engage in imperative exchanges in good faith: we know it's all just rationalization. My concept of "imperative interrogativity" (which seems to me interchangeable or perhaps complementary with "interrogative imperativity") is an attempt to answer the question: what, in grammatical terms, comes after imperative exchange? There must still be some kind of exchange with the center, but giving a part of oneself, or a part of the community, is no longer adequate. One must give everything—even sacrificing one's first born is a kind of "cheating." If I give everything, devote and donate myself completely to the center, what can I ask the center give in return? The center can supply me with the means for deferring imperative exchanges, helping us liberate ourselves from the logic of sacrifice. Rather than the articulation of two imperatives, this involves the articulation of an imperative and an interrogative: my request of the center is to remind me to pose for myself the question, "what imperative exchange is to be deferred (and reinscribed as a donation to the center) here?" This concept implies a massive cultural and moral transformation that may have been initiated by Jesus's "radicalization" of the tradition of Israelite prophecy (and in other ways in other traditions) but is far from complete. Imperative interrogativity initiates the moral and intellectual possibilities that follow from becoming increasingly adept at and committed to anticipating and "rerouting" what I call here "violent centralization." The question is how to pre-empt violent centralization by creating new forms of naming-as-commemoration.

Internal scene of representation: This is a concept of Eric Gans's that I reject. Gans assumes, I think, that there must be some subjective space where events are processed and decisions made. So, it would make sense to see the external scene upon which the sign is generated as replicated in an internal scene—this, in turn would support the whole vocabulary of interiority (consciousness, soul, psychology, conscience, will, and so on) that I see as products of disciplinary spaces mediating imperative exchanges. I insist that we are performative and mimetic all the way down.

Kingship, Divine and Sacred: I first came across the concept of "sacral kingship" from Francis Oakley's *The Politics of Enchantment*. Oakley calls sacral kingship "the political commonsense of humankind." Sacral kingship solved the problem of how to organize the social order around a humanly occupied center, but this solution was unsustainable for the same reason that sacrificial logics are unsustainable. The hypothesis I constructed from this conclusion is that the problem provisionally and limitedly solved by sacral kingship has still not been solved, and yet remains the problem of human order. One could say that the problem will have been solved once we are no longer compelled to keep simultaneously simulating and resenting sacral kingship, which is all that we have done since, even with our democratically elected presidents and prime ministers. The distinction between sacral and divine kingship I take from David Graeber and Marhsall Sahlin's *On Kings*, but my use of the distinction no doubt differs from theirs in ways I haven't tracked. Divine Kingship, in my usage, refers to the kind of monarchy we see in the ancient empires, where the king is theologically sanctified but is no longer sacrificed. I see divine kingship as the beginning of desacralization, as divine kingship is impossible without conquest, mass slavery and dispossession of local cults, which places masses of people outside of the sacred order.

Linguistic presence: The is a crucial concept from Eric Gans's *The Origin of Language*. Linguistic presence is the use of signs to ensure we remain within a shared attentional space. Gans uses the concept to account for the transition from one speech form to another (ostensive to imperative to interrogative to declarative). The imperative emerges from an "inappropriate ostensive"—someone refers to an object that isn't there, so the other interlocutor fetches it as if he had been commanded to do so. This is how the imperative is invented (or discovered). Why, exactly, does the interlocutor fetch the object? Because the alternative would be to have the sign fail, and the failure of the sign threatens violence and social chaos. I stretch the concept further, pursuing the implication that much of human inventiveness and creativity must result from attempts to maintain linguistic presence when signs are in danger of failing.

Logocentrism: "Logocentrism" is, of course, one of Jacques Derrida's signature concepts. For Derrida, it refers to the reduction within Western though of writing to a direct representation of speech, which also reduced speech to the speakers "self-presence" or intentionality. For Derrida, logocentrism suppressed what is central to writing—that it involves difference and distance. To put it simply, the text can't mean the same thing to the writer and all its readers (and the writer is himself one of the readers); the text is a tissue of other texts and no individual can hold all of the "threads." My use of David Olson's theory of writing and especially his concept of the "metalanguage of literacy" is aimed, at part, in grounding logocentrism anthropologically and historically in a way Derrida and his deconstructionist successors were unable to.

Metalanguage of literacy: This is a concept from David Olson's *The Mind on Paper*, which is in a sense a "sequel" to his much more wide-ranging *The World on Paper*. According to Olson, writing has to represent not simply speech (what was actually said) but an entire speech situation. That is, everything in a speech situation that contributes to meaning—tone, context, gesture, the social relations between the interlocutors, and so on—has to be represented by words in the written text. We would have to imagine that in a completely oral culture, one person reporting the words of another ("he said…") would simply imitate the way that person said it but in a way that included an implicit judgment in the way it is repeated. So, if someone wants to convey that the words he is repeating are false, he might repeat them in a mocking way. You can't write in a mocking way, so you have to use a word like "claim" to distance yourself from the speech you are reporting. You have to say things like "he *supposedly* saw a lion." That "supposedly" supplements the mocking tone of voice (or mimicry) that would have been used in an oral report of the other's speech. The metalanguage of literacy is this production of supplements to the oral speech situation. Once we have a word like "supposedly," we can turn it into a noun and we have "supposition." Once we have "suppositions," "assumptions," "implications," "suggestions," and so on, we also need a location to "deposit" them, and this location becomes the "mind" or the "intellect," which now is transformed into an object we can study: we can ask all kinds of questions regarding how we arrive at, how we maintain, how we use, how we revise and reject, and so on, our suppositions, assumptions, beliefs, and so on. All the disciplines that arise from these questions are products of this metalanguage of literacy. I'm using Olson's concept (in ways I doubt he would endorse) to provide a means of creating disciplinary spaces within the disciplines, so as ultimately to transform the entire field of human studies.

Mimism: "Mimism" is the foundational concept of Marcel Jousse's anthropology. Jousse is one of the great discoverers of the world of oral culture in the 20th century and in a way the most radical and consistent—and, the most clearly convergent with the mimetic theory of Girard and Gans. For Jousse, we are mimers, or imitators, all the way down (our every gesture or reaction must be learned, and how else other than by imitating?) and all the way up (our "highest" intellectual, aesthetic and spiritual pursuits are also "mimisms," the repetition—with variations, of course—of traditions that have been transmitted through imitation—how else?—for ages). "Mimism" allows us to replace questions about how people "think," what are their "values," what do they "believe," and so on—that whole "inner" world—with questions regarding how one set of practices repeats, reproduces, revises and rehearses other sets of practices. If we keep in mind that no imitation can ever be "perfect," this approach enables us to account for the whole diversity of human activity and organization.

Omnicentrism: This is a concept Gans introduces near the end of *Originary Thinking*. It's a kind of riposte to the then popular postmodern concept of "decentering"—for Gans, even decentering doesn't go far enough; every sign user must become a center in himself. I accept the descriptive accuracy of the concept—this does follow from desacralization and the general possibility that a human can occupy the center—while insisting that there is always a hierarchy of centers. Insofar as each of us is a center, we are "satellites" of some governing center.

Onomastic pedagogy: This refers to a pedagogy of naming, which is the most fundamental form of teaching and learning: pointing to something and saying, "this is_____." When we study something and try to instruct each other, what concerns us is how things should be named. We name things so that we all know we are talking about and looking at and listening to the same thing. This is ultimately the most important responsibility of the central authority—to govern is to name, and to name is to ensure that what is named has a place within the system.

Operator of negation: This is the concept Eric Gans uses in *The Origin of Language* to account for the kind of "negative ostensive" that would be the first proto-declarative sentence. "Operator of negation" is a term within logic, but I can't say anything more about that. It is important in our context because Gans uses it to refer to the kind of open-ended prohibition (like "don't smoke") that occupies a kind of middle ground between the imperative (which must be obeyed or defied within the temporal frame of the imperative itself—if I say "pass me the salt" you haven't complied with my request if you move the salt towards where I was sitting hours later, after I've gone to sleep) and the declarative, which creates a "reality" that is taken to subsist beyond any particular utterance.

Ostensive-imperative world: The ostensive and imperative signs constitute a kind of loop: once we are looking at the same thing we can request, and if the request is complied with we can confirm that by repeating the name of the thing. Eric Gans, in *The Origin* *of Language*, uses the relation between surgeon and nurse to illustrate an ostensive-imperative dialectic: the surgeon requests the "scalpel," and the nurse passes it to him, repeating, "scalpel." We can think of this as a self-contained world in which we are in direct contact with others and with objects, and where practices are, we could say, self-confirming. We could think of it as a world into which questions don't enter and where knowledge is tacit. The concept certainly overlaps with attempts within philosophy and other disciplines to distinguish more intuitive, habitual or unconscious regions of human being from those regions made explicit and available through concepts and conscious manipulation. I wanted to distinguish the ostensive-imperative "world" from the declarative "order," because the relation between this "world" and this "order" is central to the new understanding of human being I am trying to initiate here.

Semantic primes: This is Anna Wierzbicka's term for those words, identified by her and her fellow inquirers through decades of research, that have exact equivalents in every language.

Signifying center: It is necessary to distinguish between the "signifying center" and the "occupied center." On the originary scene we assume there is, literally, a physical object, most likely a carcass resulting from a successful hunt. But it's clearly not "just" a dead animal, or a meal. It has been invested with the power to compel the assembly of the group into a community around this central object. The dual nature of the center characterizes all centers, including those political centers occupied by a human (a king, a president, a prime minister, and so on). It is because the center signifies that we care about and listen to the figure at the center. How do we know what the center signifies? It must be whatever best enables us to remain assembled around it. This is, needless to say, not self-evident; rather, it is the subject matter of all of our conversations, discussions and discourses. As with the concept of the "imperative gap" (the two concepts are complementary), the purpose of this concept is to instruct us that we should know that we are always talking about how we need to interact so as to preserve the center and maximize its authority, rather than trying to subordinate the center to some external "principle" (or subversive imperative). Such attempts really aim at controlling or replacing the center, and the center certainly can't be telling you to do that.

Sparagmos: the sparagmos is an anthropological term used to refer to the consumption of the ritual object. For Eric Gans, it is a "moment" upon the originary scene, following the initial emission of the originary sign, and then followed by the proto-ritualistic reciprocal acknowledgement of the new group, mediated by the sign. Gans has spoken of the sparagmos in terms of the release of the resentment generated by the orignary scene—the violence suppressed there is "unleashed" upon the object, implying that the consumption following the creation of the sign is in a sense more violent than the more animalistic form of consumption would have been. What I add to this is the hypothesis that the sparagmos must also be where the sign is rehearsed and refined as it is used as a way of preventing the sparagmatic violence from becoming "excessive" and undoing the work of the sign.

Super-sovereignty: "Super-sovereignty" is really my translation of "imperium in imperio." Since the concept is so central to post-liberalism in the wake of Mencius Moldbug's work, I thought we should use it in our own languages. "Super-sovereignty," with its echoing of "superhero," provides an appropriately derisive connotation. The imperium in imperio is, in the first instance, the compromising of sovereign authority with the attribution of sovereignty to another authority within the same system. So, for example, who is sovereign in the US—the president? The Supreme Court? Congress? The Constitution? Once we start questioning, on the assumption that there can be only one sovereign, things can get very complicated—is the media sovereign? The "narrative"? and so on. "Super-sovereignty" shifts the question from some actual figure to the disciplinary conceptual authority invoked in order to assail (or qualify, obstruct, modify, etc.) any exercise of sovereignty. Someone has to invoke the concept, but in doing so is less claiming to exercise sovereignty than laying conditions under which we would "recognize" the "legitimacy" of the author of sovereign acts or, on the contrary, withdraw our "consent" until it can be delivered to some authority deemed legitimate. So, the president, congress, the courts (I don't know about the "media") can carry out sovereign acts (we don't, then, have to decide who is, in the last instance, sovereign) with some invocation of the super-sovereignty enabling it. All questions regarding the locus of sovereignty are not thereby settled—as always, the purpose is to replace a vocabulary that facilitates and multiplies the confusions generated by the liberal order with a vocabulary that has us looking for an enduring order even within the liberal one.

PROPOSED AND EXPERIMENTALLY SUPPORTED SEMANTIC PRIMES

CATEGORY	PRIMES					
Substantives	I	YOU	SOMEONE/PERSON	PEOPLE		
	SOMETHING/THING	BODY				
Relational Substantives			KIND	PART		
Determiners	THIS	THE SAME	OTHER			
Quantifiers	ONE	TWO	SOME	ALL	MANY/MUCH	
Evaluators	GOOD	BAD				
Descriptors	BIG	SMALL				
Mental/Experiential Predicates	THINK	KNOW	WANT	FEEL	SEE	HEAR
Speech	SAY	WORDS	TRUE			
Actions and Events	DO	HAPPEN	MOVE			
Existence and Possession	THERE IS/EXIST	HAVE				
Life and Death	LIVE	DIE				
Time	WHEN/TIME	NOW	BEFORE	AFTER	A LONG TIME	A SHORT TIME
	FOR SOME TIME	MOMENT				
Space	WHERE/PLACE	HERE	ABOVE	BELOW	FAR	NEAR
	SIDE	INSIDE	TOUCH (CONTACT)			
Logical Concepts	NOT	MAYBE	CAN	BECAUSE	IF	
Intensifier, Augmentor	VERY	MORE				
Similarity	LIKE/WAY					

NSM SEMANTIC PRIMES

I, YOU	HERE	NOW
I don't know, I want you to do/ know something, something bad can happen to me/you, someone like me	something is happening here now	something is happening here now
SOMEONE	PLACE~WHERE	TIME~WHEN
this someone, the same someone, someone else, this other someone	(in) this place, (in) the same place, somewhere else, (in) this other place, in some places, in many places, in the place where …	(at) this time, (at) the same time, at another time, at this other time, at some times, at many times, at the time when …
SOMETHING~THING	PART	KIND
this thing, the same thing, something else, this other something	this part, the same part, another part, this other part, part of something, part of someone's body, part of a place, this thing- has two/many parts	this kind, the same kind, another kind, this other kind, something/someone of one/two/ many kinds, people of one/two/ many kinds
PEOPLE	BODY	WORDS
many people, some people, people think like this, people can say	part of someone's body, two kinds of bodies, body of one kind	many words, other words, one word, say something with (not with) words, say these words, these words say something
THIS~IT	THE SAME	OTHER~ELSE
this someone (something), these people, at this time, in this place, this kind, this part, because of this, it is like this	the same someone, the same thing, the same part, the same kind, at the same time, in the same place, someone says/ does/thinks/knows/wants/feels the same	someone else, something else, at another time, somewhere else, other parts, other kinds, this other part, this other kind, this other someone, this other thing
ALL	ONE	MUCH~MANY
all people, all things, all parts, all kinds, at all times, in all places	one someone, one thing, one part, one kind, one of these things/people, something of one kind, at one time, in one place, one more thing	many people, many things, many parts, many kinds, at many times, in many places much something of this kind (e.g. water), much/many more
SOME	TWO	LITTLE~FEW
some people, some things, some parts, some kinds, at some times, in some places, some of these things/people	two things, two parts, two kinds, two of these things/people, two more things	few people, few things, a little something of this kind (e.g. water)
GOOD	BAD	TRUE
something good, someone good, good people, something good happens, do something good (for someone), feel something good, this is good, it is good if …	something bad, bad people, something bad happens, do something bad (to someone), feel something bad, this is bad, it is bad if …	this is true, this is not true
BIG	SMALL	VERY
something big, a big place, a big part	something small, a small place, a small part	very big, very small, very good, very bad, very far, very near, a very short time, a very long time

HAPPEN	DO	SAY
something happens, something happens to someone, something happens to something, something happens in a place	someone does something (to someone else), someone does something to something (with something else), someone does something with someone else, someone does something good for someone else	someone says something (to someone), someone says something (good/bad) (about someone/something), someone says something like this: "—", someone says something (not) with words
WANT	FEEL	THINK
someone wants something, someone wants to do/know/say something, someone wants someone else to do/know something, someone wants something to happen	someone feels something (good/bad) (in part of the body), someone feels like this, someone feels something good/bad towards someone else	someone thinks (something good/bad) about someone/something, someone thinks like this: "—", many people think like this: "—", (at this time) someone thinks that ...
SEE	HEAR	KNOW
someone sees someone/something (in a place)	someone hears something	someone knows something (about someone/something), someone knows when/where/who ..., someone knows that ..., people can know this, someone knows someone else (well)
BE (specificational)	THERE IS	MOVE
this someone is someone like me, this is something of one kin, this is something big/small, someone can say who this someone is, someone can say what kind of thing this is ...	there is something in this place, there is someone in this place, there are two/many kinds of ...	someone moves (in this place), something moves in this place, parts of this someone's body move
BE (locational)	HAVE	TOUCH
someone is in a place, something is in a place, someone is with someone else	someone has something (many things), someone has something of this kind	something touches something else (in a place), something touches someone (part of this someone's body), someone touches someone else (part of this other someone's body)
LIVE	DIE	MORE~ANYMORE
someone lives for a long time, someone lives in this place, many people live in this place, someone lives with someone else	someone dies at this time, all people die at some time	someone wants more, someone does more, someone wants to know/say more about it, one more, two more, many more, not living anymore, not like this anymore

NOT~DON'T	CAN	BECAUSE
I don't know, I don't want this, someone can't do this, it is not like this, not good, not bad, not because of anything else	someone can (can't) do something, someone can't not do something, something (good/bad) can happen, it can be like this	because of this/it, it happened because this someone did something before
LIKE~WAY	MAYBE	IF
do it like this, move like this, happen like this, do it in this way, think like this: "—", it is like this: …, like/as this someone wants, someone like me	maybe it is like this, maybe it is not like this, maybe someone else can do it	if it happens like this for some time …, if you do this …, if someone does something like this …
BEFORE	A SHORT TIME	FOR SOME TIME
before this, some time before, a short time before, a long time before	for a short time, a short time before, a short time after	it happens for some time, someone does this for some time
AFTER	A LONG TIME	MOMENT
after this, some time after, a short time after, a long time after	for a long time, a long time before, a long time after	it happens in one moment
ABOVE	NEAR	INSIDE
above this place	near this place, near someone	inside this something, inside part of someone's body
BELOW	FAR	ON ONE SIDE
below this place	far from this place	on this side, on the same side, on one side, on two sides, on all sides

Natural Semantic Metalanguage (NSM)

Semantic primes are the vocabulary of the Natural Semantic Metalanguage. NSM grammar specifies how primes can be combined in ways that make sense and appear to be possible in all languages. This table displays the English exponents of the primes and some of their basic combinatorial possibilities. Many other, more complex combinations are possible, especially using operators and connectives like NOT, CAN, MAYBE, IF, and BECAUSE, and drawing on the complement-taking properties of KNOW, WANT and THINK. Primes can have two or more exponents (allolexes) in a given language, e.g. *other* and *else* in English. In some languages certain combinations of primes are expressed by a portmanteau, e.g. in Polish the combination 'like this' is expressed by a single word *tak*.

Chart by Cliff Goddard, Griffith University, Queensland, Australia.